Wisdom With
Understanding
is Better
Than Rubies

Lurine Karon Greenberg
Fine Arts Collection

PORTRAIT

ALSO BY WILLIAM S. MCFEELY

Proximity to Death

Sapelo's People: A Long Walk into Freedom

Frederick Douglass

Grant: A Biography

Yankee Stepfather: General O. O. Howard and the Freedmen

Ulysses S. Grant: An Album (with Neil Giordano)

Thomas Eakins at Age Thirty-five to Forty, c. 1879–84.
(Pennsylvania Academy of the Fine Arts)

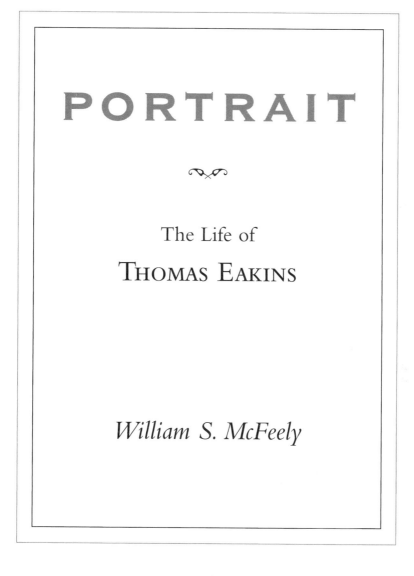

PORTRAIT

The Life of

THOMAS EAKINS

William S. McFeely

W. W. NORTON & COMPANY

New York London

For information about permission to reproduce selections from this book, write to Permissions,
W. W. Norton & Company, Inc., 500 Fifth Avenue, New York, NY 10110

Manufacturing by RR Donnelley, Harrisonburg, VA
Book design by Anna Oler

Library of Congress Cataloging-in-Publication Data

McFeely, William S.
Portrait : the life of Thomas Eakins / William S. McFeely
p. cm.
Includes bibliographical references and index.
ISBN-13: 978-0-393-05065-3 (hardcover)
ISBN-10: 0-393-05065-3 (hardcover)
1. Eakins, Thomas, 1844–1916. 2. Painters—United States—Bibliography. I. Eakins, Thomas,
1844–1916. II. Title.
ND237.E15 2006
759.13—dc22
[B]   2006021283

W. W. Norton & Company, Inc.
500 Fifth Avenue, New York, N.Y. 10110
www.wwnorton.com

W. W. Norton & Company Ltd.
Castle House, 75/76 Wells Street, London W1T 3QT

1 2 3 4 5 6 7 8 9 0

Philip Hamburger
In memoriam

Eakins has always spoken to me in a personal and peculiar way.

CONTENTS

PREFACE

"It's Too Real"

In Rome's Palazzo Pamphilij, in a small red room, alone with the Bernini bust of the pope, is one of the world's great paintings, Diego Velázquez's portrait of Innocent X. His compelling face suggests both malice and stupidity, his big ears are as the artist pitilessly saw them.[1] The gorgeousness of scarlet silk atop a drift of white confirms the seated Innocent's papal authority, but the whole of it brought forth his *e troppo vero*.[2]

Visiting Madrid's Prado in 1868, Thomas Eakins would not have seen this painting by Velázquez, but he learned more one morning looking at the seventeenth-century artist's other work than he was to learn from any other source. Eakins went on to become perhaps America's finest realist, but it was only when he pushed reality to an almost painful point that he reached true greatness.

The Eakins painting that first haunted me years ago was Smith College's *Mrs. Edith Mahon*. I knew nothing about the sitter, but I could not stop staring. There is the expanse of the flesh of her chest, the still beautiful face, the relentless eyes, and, above all, the inexpressible sadness of that face. Could I discern as much about the painter as about his subject in that unforgettably sad face?

PORTRAIT

Mrs. Edith Mahon, 1904. (Smith College Museum of Art)
See color plate 1.

INTRODUCTION

THE RICH, sweet smell of linseed oil perfumed the attic room. Like toy soldiers on parade, stalagmites of pigment crowded the table to his left. Holding his brush firmly, he took a confident swipe at a corner of the sea of scrambled color on the board. Scrubbing with the brush, he added a little ochre, a bit of blue—then reached to squeeze out more and more white. The weather was cooperating; from the window, daylight lit the right side of Edith Mahon and made him see anew the startling expanse of the flesh of her chest rising from its frame of black lace and velvet. Swiftly he brought the brush to the canvas and the splendid flesh emerged. As he hunched over his easel, his relentless eye moved up to the face, to the strong nose, firmly closed lips—finally the eyes. Deftly, with a smaller brush and the marriage of still more colors, he painted her lustrous eyes. The right one, in the light, has the hint of a tear forming.

In 1904, Thomas Eakins gave us a beautiful woman, not in celebrity magazine terms, but one rich in ineffable sadness. Edith Mahon is said not to have liked the picture; there was too much sadness exposed for her to have felt otherwise. She was an Englishwoman, a talented pianist who, in Philadelphia, won some recognition as an accompanist to important soloists and as a teacher of the piano. It is altogether fitting that she was part of the circle of musicians Eakins knew and that hers was a face he was drawn to. The disgrace of a divorce was upon her when Eakins painted the portrait; she returned to England and died not long afterward.

Eakins was as ruthlessly hard on himself when he painted his own portrait in 1902; he was too honest a painter not to record what he saw. As he left the nineteenth century behind him, a century that had once held such promise for him—and for his America—he was disheartened, even despairing. When he was born in 1844, his America was the city of Philadelphia and a quiet protected part of the city at that. Nothing, it would seem, stood in his way. What changed?

As a historian, I am often dismayed by what change brings, but never surprised by it. Much as I admire the insight of art historians, I find that in many of their studies of Eakins, they see a static artist, even as the paintings change. Change in a person's life is seldom a matter of a single moment; Thomas Eakins was no Saul on the road to Damascus; there are even signs of what the change brought about before the crucial moment in his life. In the early indoor pictures of his sisters, Frances and Margaret, painted soon after his return from Europe in a household overshadowed by their mother's madness, there is a foretelling of the strength and anguish that he would find later in his career.

In these paintings of the young women, there is more than a hint of Eakins' ability to see the poignant sadness in the faces of some of the people he portrayed later in his career. When he went outdoors, the young man, an athlete, took part in the sports he depicted with exuberance—men in boats under sail, at bat, or bent to the wonderful exhaustion of rowing.

Writers should not have an exclusive hold on conceiving of a better world. There were many authors in the nineteenth century who did so conceive. When Henry David Thoreau wrote, "The mass of men live lives of quiet desperation,"[1] he had hopes that their emotional economy could tally to something better. As we shall see, Thomas Eakins, not a man of words, but of pictures, shared such vision when he painted the last of his pictures of the outdoors. *Swimming* was his *Walden*.

The Writing Master (Portrait of Benjamin Eakins), 1882.
(Metropolitan Museum of Art, New York)
See color plate 2.

I

AN ARTIST'S FATHER

THOMAS EAKINS HAD an unorthodox father. Rather than warn his son that being an artist was a depraved way of life ensuring poverty, Benjamin Eakins thought an artist son was a fine idea. Benjamin was a second-generation Irish American who moved into Philadelphia from rural Pennsylvania; in 1843 he married Caroline Cowperthwait. Thomas, their first child, was born the next year. A calligrapher and writing master, neither the most lucrative of callings, Benjamin somehow managed to provide his artist son with the lifelong wherewithal to paint without regard to whether he sold a canvas or didn't. This was a great luxury, but for Benjamin's long life it also imposed a remarkable measure of psychological and financial authority by the father over the son. It entailed no sacrifice on Benjamin Eakins' part; there were funds enough for vacations at the shore and an extended trip to Europe for him and his daughter Margaret.

Benjamin Eakins relished the role of paterfamilias, keeping gentle control of his wife, his son, and Margaret, who never married, in the family home. The tall, three-story brick house at 1729 Mt. Vernon

Eakins at about age six, c. 1850.
Photographer unknown. (Courtesy of the
Pennsylvania Academy of the Fine Arts,
Philadelphia, Bregler Collection)

Street, in the near north side of Philadelphia, was surrounded by other
brick row houses accented by white stone steps. The Eakinses' inner
door was framed in a vine pattern of colored glass. There was a generous parlor to the left, behind which were the dining room and kitchen.
At the rear of the third floor was the spacious room that would be
Thomas Eakins' studio; light entered from windows on three sides, out
back was the tiny coveted city garden. The house was often full of
daughters, their spouses, grandchildren, occasional other relatives—and
a zoo's worth of semidomesticated fauna.

As ebullient as was Benjamin Eakins, Thomas's mother, Caroline
Cowperthwait Eakins was taciturn. (In the Eakins story, don't look for
much twenty-first-century ethnic diversity in this sea of British names.)
Caroline was born into a Philadelphia Quaker family; her father was an
upholsterer working at home at 4 Carrollton Square, just outside the

1729 Mt. Vernon Street, Philadelphia. (Library of Congress)

city center. The narrow two-story house—referred to in the local vernacular as "a door and two windows wide"—must have been crowded when, in 1843, Caroline came home with her groom. It was more crowded still after three babies were born to the couple. Benjamin and Caroline lived with Caroline's parents and grandparents until 1850, when they moved to a place of their own, around the corner on Green Street. In 1857, after two years in another Green Street house, Benjamin bought 1729 Mt. Vernon Street. All three of the Eakins houses, scarcely any distance from one another, were on respectably middle-class streets a quarter of a mile north of the more fashionable and commercial streets of central Philadelphia.

The Mt. Vernon house, near the corner of 20th Street, was home to Eakinses for three-quarters of a century. Thomas Eakins left only twice in his life—for the three and a half years he spent in Europe, and for three years when he married and moved downtown to an apartment and studio at 1330 Chestnut Street. The couple was back at 1729 in 1887. They outlived all of the other inhabitants, bearing witness to the deaths of Caroline, Margaret, Aunt Eliza, and Benjamin.

A gifted calligrapher, Benjamin Eakins probably had thoughts of an artistic career himself. He was a master at his craft who, among other commissions, made diplomas for the University of Pennsylvania. Unlike other skilled artisans—furniture makers or skillful weavers—Benjamin was in direct contact with the well-educated administrators of the university. His position as teacher of penmanship at the excellent Friends Central School, which he held for fifty-one years, put him in the company of teachers and promising students. Not only were these positions breadwinners, they invited friendships with intellectuals. Thomas grew up in this world and was similarly at ease with people with a variety of scholarly interests.

Father and son were equally at home with athletes outdoors. The grasses of the vast South Jersey marshes are in brilliant green in the spring and early summer. Stretching far inland was some of the richest of farming soil, soil green with vegetables that sold to markets of eastern towns and cities. Tom Eakins and his father would venture into this peaceful rural world just after school closed for the summer, taking the ferry to Camden and the Jersey Central to Bridgeton, then a spur down to Fairton.

Benjamin was a close friend of Abigail and Samuel Williams and their farmhouse would be the first stopping place for Benjamin and Tom. Then, well-fed, father and son would head to their primitive cabin, the Fish House, to ready themselves for hunting rail, a small secretive bird. For next to nothing, they would employ a black neighbor who would pole their long shallow boat into the marshes, moving as quickly and quietly as possible, stirring just enough to flush the rail into the air. (A man in the rear would skillfully keep the boat still and level so that the gunner could stand and take his shot.) Tom's love of swimming meant hours in the nearby Cohansey river.

In all, the families had wonderfully peaceful vacations in this South Jersey country. The Williamses' eldest daughter, Mary Adeline—always called Addie—became a great friend of the second Eakins child, Frances, known as Fanny. When the women of the family accompanied the two men to Fairton, they stayed at the Williams house. Later Addie, studying in Philadelphia, stayed with the Eakinses. The Williams house was the civilized stop on the trips to the Cohansey. The male domain was the Fish House, used first by Tom and his father; later by Tom and Samuel Murray, his student and close friend. It was their haven from the world.

The physical legacy of father to son was apparent. Benjamin Eakins was a handsome man whose stocky, muscular physique Thomas, taller and equally well-built, inherited. It was in the emotional realm that the two differed markedly. The difference between them is suggested not in physique, but in their faces. When his father was well along in years, Tom painted an affectionate portrait of him at his desk, pen in hand. Here and in the many photographs of him that exist, Benjamin displays a serenity denied Thomas. In many photographs of Eakins' face as well in the superb painting by Susan Eakins and in his own late self-portrait, serenity is utterly absent. Whatever sunlight the father had been able to shed on his son, the son had his own darkness.

Eakins' mother wore her own far deeper darkness. The details of Caroline Cowperthwait Eakins' life are scant. She bore five children. Tom, the eldest, was born on July 25, 1844. Over the next twenty years, Caroline Eakins had four more children: Fanny in 1848; a second son, Benjamin, who died as an infant; Margaret in 1853; and, in 1865, when she was forty-five, Caroline, or Caddy. (by then Tom was a young man in art school). This last pregnancy, late in life, may have exaggerated the mother's already precarious mental health.

Tom inherited his mother's dark hair and rather sallow complexion, and her dark piercing eyes, but how he fared with her emotionally is difficult to say. It is hard to measure how steady a hand she held out to her son, but, as we shall see, when she needed steadying, Eakins was there. There is ample affection and companionability in his letters from Paris—Tom tells her that in the throes of hideous seasickness, "I dreamed that although sick, my head was on your lap"—and rich details of his trip. Her letters to him are lost.[1]

The nature of Caroline's mental instability, which was later to become acute, might have had a genetic component. One granddaughter shared the malady. Tom's depression, hard to diagnose from the vantage point of a century, was recurrent and it might have owed something to inheritance, although it seems to me that you can cook up a good case of depression without more than a dash of genes. This latter possibility flies in the face of present-day fashion; as one dissenting biologist puts it disparagingly, "there is at present, no aspect of social or individual life that is not claimed for the genes."[2]

My sense is that Tom's depression was of a different order from the mental illness that destroyed both his mother and his niece. As one expert has said, depression, as a debilitating, but not lethal, condition, is "by its nature episodic."[3] There are now medical therapies that reduce the worst effects of depression; in Eakins' time, there were not, but there was an understanding of the condition and a way was found for him to cope with a particularly damaging episode. I do not mean by this that the depression was made to disappear, but rather that it was put back on its usual course of highs and lows. Depression can have its virtues. Familiar with the condition, Eakins was able to sense it in many of the people whose portraits he painted.

There was no such malaise apparent in the paintings of Benjamin Eakins playing chess or at work on a diploma. Benjamin's calligraphy commissions and the school payroll cannot have provided the wherewithal for the lifetime financial needs of an artist, but provision there was. Clearly there were funds from another source. Sometime before the purchase in 1857 of the Mt. Vernon Street house and certainly before paying for Thomas's sojourn in Paris a decade later, Benjamin accumulated a substantial amount of money. With shrewd guesses rather than the discovery of any record, one historian credits Benjamin Eakins with timely investments in railroads, particularly appropriate for someone in the city that was the home to the powerful Pennsylvania Railroad. Another guess, supported by a few records of holdings, was that time-honored route to comfortable middle-class security, shrewd investments in real estate.[4] There is a telling bit of negative evidence in the remarkable records of the credit-evaluating companies at the Harvard Business School. Often these cases of small business investors are the story of nineteenth-century men ruined by borrowing, and eventually failing. There is no record there of any borrowing, or attempt to do so, by Benjamin Eakins.[5]

The house at 1729 Mt. Vernon Street was sizable, and a good thing too. When Fanny married in 1872, she and her husband, William Crowell, moved in briefly. Caddy did the same thirteen years later, when she married Frank Stephens. Assorted other relatives were there from time to time, including Tom's bespectacled favorite aunt, Eliza Cowperthwait (her beguiling smile endures in her photograph), to say nothing of the dogs and monkey and pet rat and no end of others.

What was the nature of the relationship of the two men, father and son? If Benjamin Eakins took vicarious pleasure in his son's ability, did the calligrapher resent the fact that his son had surpassed him? One realm in which Benjamin was not to be outdone was sports; Tom was an able athlete, but the father was his superior. If Thomas as a young man was good in a single scull, Benjamin in his forties raced in a two-man shell with his son's classmate and the Philadelphia champion, Max Schmitt. Rather than creating a competitive clash, Benjamin's sportsmanship brought the two men together. They sailed, hunted rail, and famously and furiously bicycled together all over their city. Benjamin Eakins appreciated his son, understood him, and laid firm claim to him for the rest of his long life.

The two teamed up to see to it that Thomas got a superior education at a remarkable public school, Central High School. Producing citizens of sound republican virtue was the aim of the school. Meritocracy was the guiding principle; students of undoubted scholarly merit were required. Benjamin Eakins knew a good many people in Philadelphia and knew too that meritocracy could receive a head start by getting a child into the best schools. Benjamin knew the ropes; Tom took care of the other half of the equation by working hard and with enthusiasm. He had plenty of talent to bring to the enterprise.

The Champion Single Sculls (Max Schmitt in a Single Scull), 1871.
(Metropolitan Museum of Art, New York)

II

Central High School

LEARNING HIS ABCs at home, Tom attended the Zane Street Grammar School, where he got so excellent a start on his education that, on graduating, he could aspire to a place in Central High School. It is not accurate to judge what can be learned in schools by whether they call themselves a "high school," a "college," or a "university." This was certainly so in mid-nineteenth-century America, when there was then only a sketchy concept of formal progression toward professional credentials. In terms of a firm grasp on the essentials of intellect, "high schools" like the Latin Schools in Boston and nearby Roxbury and Philadelphia's Central High School did as thorough a job as many institutions with grander-sounding names. Affectionately (and not inaccurately) known as the "People's College," Central High was one of the leading educational institutions in the country, on any level.[1]

Public schools came early to Philadelphia, with grammar schools established in 1818. In 1836, to dispose of surpluses in the treasury, the federal government gave sufficient funds to Philadelphia to build Central High School.[2] The cornerstone of the tall, three-story federal-style building was laid in September 1837 on the site of City Hall.[3] In Philadelphia, Benjamin Franklin looks over every shoulder and, fittingly, Central High was founded by his great-grandson, Alexander Dallas Bache.[4] Educated at West Point, Bache briefly taught engineering there after his graduation. In the days before the strict hierarchy in education, he moved comfortably to a professorship in natural philosophy and chemistry at the University of Pennsylvania. It was not a step down when, in 1837, he was named president of Central High School.

Bache had plentiful public money to work with and ambitious plans. He assembled what was the first substantial school library of one thousand books and a rigorous course of study was devised.[5] It is still a mark of pride that at the outset the school's astronomy equipment was superior to that of Harvard; shortly, it was the fifth institution in the country to have a permanent observatory. The teachers at Central were known as "professor," with no sense that this was a misuse of the term; the men were all well-known in their fields. The degree they were authorized to grant was bachelor of arts, which, on graduation, Eakins was awarded.

Central High was a product of the reform movement of the 1830s and '40s, when the nation sought to hand over the responsibilities for the republic from the aristocratic few to the broader populace. The Constitution had been the creation of the elect, who expected that men of similar virtue would govern. The problem was that the Declaration of Independence promised that all men should share in the nation's blessings. With the advent of the nineteenth century, citizens set out to see to this. There was an organization for every cause: antislavery, women's rights, prison reform, temperance, and schools for all.

The early records of Central High School show that the students, all white and male, were from the "proprietary" middle class, presumably from families with their own businesses, but extending to the "employed" middle class, the "skilled worker" class, and, significantly, boys from the "unskilled worker" class.[6] The declared goal of the public institution was to prepare its graduates for productive positions in the community; but Central High School, like other superior urban public

Central High School, Philadelphia.
(Library Company of Philadelphia, Brenner Collection)

high schools in American cities, provided a way up in society, and a great many of its graduates seized that opportunity. From Thomas Eakins' time to ours, obituaries of impressive judges, dedicated high school principals—indeed, men who succeeded in a wide range of callings— tell of how the boy (until recently, it would be a boy), coming from a relatively simple background, began his rise at Townsend Harris in New York or Boston Latin or Philadelphia's Central High.

Admission to the school was highly competitive. Ninety-nine percent of Eakins' three-thousand-odd fellow Philadelphia grammar school graduates weren't even recommended by their principals for admission to Central High. Of those who had the requisite grades and recommendation from their school principal, only half passed the entrance examination.

In 1857, Thomas Eakins was one who did. He joined the 516 other boys studying at Central High School, by then in a new building at Broad and Green streets, six blocks from his home.[7] In most quarters, the education of a painter is understood in terms of how he learned to take brush to pigment—what master taught him, whose work influenced his own. If the world is taken into account at all, it is only in terms of how it affected his art. This can lead us to a lopsided picture of that painter. Lloyd Goodrich, an art historian and curator, made the shrewd judgment that Alexander Jay O'Neill, a drawing teacher at Central High School, taught Eakins more than he learned in subsequent years at the Pennsylvania Academy of the Fine Arts.[8]

Goodrich, like other art historians, was interested in the development of Eakins as a painter, but focusing on O'Neill alone of Eakins' teachers at Central High tends to sell its other instructors—and Eakins—short. The scholar-teachers carried on the best tradition of educational flexibility; Eakins was the product of what we would call a fine liberal arts education. He was a superb student. It misses a critical point to see, for example, that Eakins' fluency—if sometimes doubtful accuracy—in French simply enabled him to get into the École des Beaux-Arts. His command of seven languages was not simply a matter of utility; it spoke of a strong intellect.

His later interest in anatomy was more than a tool to enable him to get a body right on canvas; his fascination with medicine did not simply enable him to paint surgeons at work in their operating amphitheaters; and his profound grasp of physics was not a matter of putting the right instrument in the hand of a physicist Eakins painted years later. Thomas Eakins had a first-rate mind that he did a first-rate job of disguising. He cannot have done justice to all he saw in a long day at the Louvre when he wrote of having seen a "lot of funny old pictures." A good many of them no doubt were. Granted, he was writing to a young sister, but he was not much more forthcoming in letters to his father, with whom he could have had a conversation by correspondence that touched on the merits of the paintings.

Tom studied Greek and Latin—Caesar, Vergil, and so on—at Central High under Professor Haverstick. His less than stellar grades in the sub-

jects may speak more to the severity of this teacher than the performance of the student. (Like other terrifying teachers, Haverstick was not
forgotten. Tom wrote to his father years later telling him that he preferred "sunlight & children & beautiful women & men," rather than
"the nasty besmeared wooden hard gloomy pictures figures" out of the
classics of "the last few centuries & Ingres & the Greek letters I learned
in High School with old Haverstick.")[9]

Whether he would have credited Professor Haverstick or not, this
training in Latin aided in his mastery of Romance languages. Eakins had
four years of rigorous training in French language and literature with
Professor Bregy—five days of recitation a week.[10] So taken with French
was he that when in Spain, he kept his diary in French and in the years
immediately after returning to the United States he wrote friends in the
language.

Once he reached Europe, Eakins, with his excellent ear, spoke the
Italian he had taught himself back in Philadelphia. On a trip to Spain,
he hired a tutor and in short order spoke good Spanish and could cor-
respond in the language, as he had been able to do in Italian. These
Romance languages would not have helped with German, but in
Philadelphia it was no rarity to encounter German. Tom's good friend
Max Schmitt, fluent in his family's original language, saw to it that Tom
spoke German comfortably before he got to Europe.

Eakins was not taken by General History; the word "general" may
have been the problem—he would have done better with specific stories of the past. (He never painted a "general" picture—wouldn't have
known what one was, if indeed, any such thing exists.) More specific
was the history of Greece and Rome, two great powers and two
republics that failed, and that of England, which had almost succeeded,
when with the Glorious Revolution of 1688, the nation limited the
power of its monarch. The English cousins had laid the groundwork for
republican virtue to triumph with the establishment of the United
States. Or so Central High's history department would have its students
believe. There was no instruction in contemporary literature;
Shakespeare was the most recent work that Central's curriculum

encompassed. In fact, philology was the mainstay of Professor Hurt's course in language; a year was spent translating "Saxon into English." A bit more practical was the requirement of a weekly composition by every student. Astronomy, Navigation, Surveying, coupled with Geometry and Trigonometry prepared Eakins for his lifelong fascination with science.[11] He converted his strength in mechanical drawing—a strength that would have equipped a skilled engineer—into a tool that enabled him to make drawings and sketches for paintings of incredible accuracy. He lined out the perspective and the measurement to the inch, before placing Max Schmitt's scull precisely on the Schuylkill.[12]

In the years ahead Eakins was the intellectual equal of the many forward-looking scientists in Philadelphia's medical institutions and at the University of Pennsylvania. Not surprisingly, Eakins excelled in his drawing classes; his drawings foretell the marriage of an artist's eye to a scientific mind. A complicated lathe is rendered in perfect detail and placed artistically on the paper. Similarly, gears, meshed and disengaged, are depicted with professional skill. But more than that, Eakins grasped not merely the forms, but their functions. To this early drawing, Eakins playfully added two tiny comical stick figures. Pursuit of good work hadn't been allowed to become totally sober; the figures are a hint of humanism in the work of one who was more than a literalist.

Graduation Day, no simple occasion, was July 11, 1861. Not even the fact that there was a war on could deter Central High School's celebration. The doors of the Academy of Music opened at nine in the morning, the ceremony began at ten. Nicholas Harper McGuire, Central High's third president, presided. Hunger must have set in by the time the eight addresses, each preceded by music from the Germania Orchestra, and the awarding of testimonials and conferring of degrees was over. There was the historical address by the "third honor," the salutatory address, and the valedictory address; "Tom C. Eakins Fourth Honor" gave the scientific address.[13]

There were levels enough for a French lycée. Maximilian Schmitt (the single-scull champion) was the third most "distinguished" in Division A, with a grade of 95.7. Tom Eakins didn't make this club; he,

The Academy of Music, Philadelphia.
(Courtesy of the Free Library of Philadelphia)

with 92.8 and another close friend, William Sartain, with 94, had to settle for "meritorious." Unstated in the program for the graduation was
the fact that these graduates would be able to speak English with what
used to be called a "cultured tongue." The graduates' photographs, standard yearbook pictures, were arranged in an oval in the printed program. So rigorous was Central High that only a quarter of those who
entered graduated.

Fuss and feathers of graduation day aside, the perceptive art historian
Elizabeth Johns had it exactly: Thomas Eakins' education prepared him
for "seeing correctly and thinking profoundly."[14] But there was a cost.
He had set so high a standard of achievement that reaching a goal of
excellence became mandatory. Or so it seemed to him. Even as he
became a superbly accomplished artist, he took the lack of recognition
as evidence that the goal had not been reached.

III

FOUR UNEVENTFUL YEARS?

IT IS DIFFICULT for an American historian to imagine nothing happening between 1861 and 1865, but for this story I may have to. I am not the first writer to despair at finding anything beyond bits and scraps and conjectures about what Thomas Eakins was up to between the age of seventeen and twenty-one. These were, after all, his coming-of-age years and, as such, ought to be replete with great—and discernable—significance. If they were, he isn't telling.

Benjamin had taught Tom to be a skilled calligrapher. If learning to draw the words exquisitely equipped the son with a craft that might have enabled him to earn his livelihood, it also did much more. It added significantly to his training as an artist. For the rest of his life, Thomas Eakins could, when the spirit moved him, write a letter, doodle in a margin, or address an impressive envelope. More important, he used the skill when he frequently put words in his paintings. His name is hidden on the stern of his scull in *Max Schmitt in a Single Scull*, on the cross in *The Cruxifixion*, and in other pictures. Carrying the urge further, Eakins perceptively "framed" his study of a physicist, *Portrait of Professor Henry*

A. Rowland, etching scientific symbols used by a physicist onto the actual frame of the canvas.[1]

After graduating from Central High at sixteen in the summer of 1861, Eakins lived at home, helping his father with his calligraphy business and perhaps teaching the craft. That fall, he did not attempt to enroll at either the University of Pennsylvania or one of the medical colleges, as his fascination with anatomy might have made logical.

If Central High School represented one goal of the republic, to educate to a high level a class of honored artisans, another institution in Philadelphia was designed to say that the new nation valued high culture as well. At the end of the eighteenth century, a group of local artists staged the country's first art show, the Columbianum. With this stimulus, the Pennsylvania Academy of the Fine Arts was founded in 1805.[2] An art museum that would declare that the republic was not without a culture, the Academy somewhat ironically sought to emulate London's Royal Academy. Biblical scenes, illustrations of moments in literature, and Benjamin West's vast historical canvases were favored over simpler American subjects. (Emerson had not yet called on his countrymen to create an original culture of their own.)

It was an Englishman, John Sartain, who sought to turn the academy's eyes toward French art. Sartain moved to Philadelphia and established himself as a central figure in the city's art world, as a highly skilled engraver. (Engraving was essential in disseminating art in an era lacking any photographic reproduction of paintings.) Sartain traveled regularly to Paris, the art center of the time, and hoped, as a director of the academy, to see to it that art instruction follow that of the École des Beaux-Arts. The Sartains were family friends of the Eakinses; Tom's schoolmate, William Sartain was John's son, and Emily, a friend of the Eakins children, his daughter.

The academy had the reputation as the nation's leading art school, though not in the structured manner of such schools today. It made do without a formal faculty. When Tom, Billy, and Emily began to study at the academy, students had studio space and could draw from casts of antique sculpture or from hired models; instruction came informally from the person at the next easel or from the professional artists who came in, fairly casually, to instruct and critique. The most prominent of these instructors was Christian Schussele, a Paris-trained artist who came from the much fought-over region of Alsace, which, in his day, was part of France.

The academy was progressive in its admission of women as students and Emily Sartain sought a career as an artist on a par with her brother and with Tom. Intellectually determined, she and Tom taught themselves Italian, read Dante together, and wrote each other charming florid letters in that Romance language. The two were devoted friends and marriage seemed to lie ahead. Meanwhile there was the business of training for a career in art. After years spent achieving technical proficiency with pencil and charcoal and gaining the necessary self-confidence, the student might begin to paint. Eakins' enrollment in the academy allowed him to attend drawing sessions as well as lectures in anatomy given by a physician "who had no great opinion of the requirements of a congregation of art students," as one of these unfondly recalled.[3] Many of those drawing at the academy were amateurs, a status held in higher regard in the nineteenth century than today. Curiously, among them were men from the university and the medical schools, either ambitious Sunday painters or, in the case of the medical men, students wanting to connect their understanding of human anatomy with an ability to draw. Samuel Gross, whom Eakins was to depict in a famous picture, drew at the academy while Eakins was a student.

Mary Cassatt, one of Schussele's students, recalled taking drawings to his private studio for a weekly evaluation of her work, adding that she was not alone in going to him for such critiques. Eakins also worked under Schussele, who saw talent in the young man. By 1866, Schussele judged his student ready to go to Paris to study at the most distinguished art institute in the world, the École des beaux-Arts.

The only defect in this tale—the progress of a Philadelphia boy on his way toward a great career—is a little matter of savage civil war only counties away from Philadelphia. For Eakins to have been oblivious of the American Civil War stretches credulity to the breaking point; Tom could scarcely walk to the academy without encountering the city's anguish over the war. There was a small but stalwart antislavery society in Philadelphia—predominantly white and Quaker. Given Benjamin's strong-minded freethinking, the family, apparently not compelled by abolitionist fervor, could have held pacific views and consciously determined that Tom should not go to war.

So-called Peace Democrats, accepting of slavery, were in control of the city government for the first two years of the war and roundly condemned Lincoln's Emancipation Proclamation of January 1, 1863. Opposing them was the equally committed Union League, fully in support of Lincoln's war after Gettysburg had ended the threat to Pennsylvania. (The league's imposing building on Broad Street remains a virtual shrine to Lincoln, Grant, and the local boy General George Gordon Meade. So grand was the clubhouse that it was easy, but erroneous, to imagine that the city as a whole was as fervent in the cause as were the league's founders.)

Tom Eakins' good friends Billy Sartain and Max Schmitt enlisted and, like any young man, Tom must have pondered if he should too. A small clue as to the Eakins family's sentiments, if not actions, lies in the work of the Sartain family. John Sartain made engravings of Peter Rothermel's heroic painting of the Battle of Gettysburg. Before his enlistment, his son William made a widely distributed engraving, *Young America Crushing Rebellion and Sedition*, an exceedingly odd depiction of a naked cherub strangling two malevolent snakes as the eagle of the Union, looking more like a turkey vulture, hovers ominously over the scene. Evidence of the Sartains' long-standing attitude toward slavery is John Sartain's engraving of the famous Nathaniel Joycelyn portrait of Cinque, the leader of the *Amistad* revolt.[4] Slaves on board a ship from Cuba had revolted, seized the boat, and brought it into port in New England. In a sensational 1841 trial in New Haven, former president John Quincy Adams argued successfully that the slaves were free now that they were in Connecticut, a state free of slavery. Cinque's release buoyed antislavery spirits; Sartain's engraving allowed the country to see a handsome black man who had rebelled.

Tom's mother's family, the Cowperthwaits, had once been Quakers, but that faith had not been carried into the Eakins household in sufficient strength to have any member describe him or herself as a Friend. Yet, a telling detail lies in a letter written thirty years later in which Eakins, explaining why no church was involved in his marriage, wrote, rebutting claims that he and his wife, Susan, were not married, that "our marriage was in the Quaker form."[5] That Thomas, his mother, and his father might have had pacific views does not seem out of character; Benjamin was teaching in a Quaker school at the time and it is hard to imagine that there was not a great deal of soul-searching over what Tom's role in respect to war should be.

Tom, like his father, was something of a freethinker and, politically, at least once the war was won, called himself a Unionist. After the war, he made it clear, in a letter bitterly critical of Andrew Johnson, that he was a Republican, but his dismay at Lincoln's successor was based not on his disregard of the rights of the freed people, but on his refusal to stand against the resurgence of political strength in once rebellious southerners.

Before the Civil War Philadelphia had been deeply divided over the question of slavery. Richard Allen, the minister of the leading black church, the Methodist Episcopal, long maintained a tie to his counterpart in the Baltimore church—Maryland, unlike Pennsylvania, was still a slaveholding state—and made Philadelphia a key stop on the Underground Railroad. This clandestine linking of slavery foes had a well-structured system for meeting, caring for, and assisting escaping slaves. However, the northern states, while lacking slavery, were not devoid of people opposed to this disregard of property; slave catchers abounded—particularly in New York City. Plans were carefully made and instructions passed along so that the traveler was met by sympathetic citizens who saw him or her off to the next person in the next city. Perhaps the most famous of slaves who made their way north was Frederick Douglass, who was passed along to New York City and ultimately to the relatively safe, Quaker-dominated city of New Bedford, Massachusetts. Even more impressive than the help given the articulate and wily Douglass was the assistance offered to Anna Murray, a free but illiterate woman on her way to marry Douglass. Free or not, she was vulnerable to predatory slave catchers who not infrequently managed to seize African Americans, slave or free, and sell them back into slavery. Unable to read even the street signs, Anna, depending on oral instructions, safely reached a free black man's house in New York City, a famous stop on the railroad. She and Douglass were married there before continuing to New Bedford.

The white board of managers of the Pennsylvania Anti-Slavery Society—which had not "yet quite rid themselves of what seems to be a prejudice against color," said Douglass with excessive tact—included one of the nation's leading abolitionists Lucretia Coffin Mott.[6]

As committed as these antislavery forces were, they were outnumbered by strident enemies of abolition—people whose opposition was not merely verbal. Six years before Eakins was born they set fire to and destroyed Pennsylvania Hall, built as an antislavery meeting place.[7] Their rabble-rousing anti-abolitionism and hatred of all black Americans had not abated during Eakins' time.

When Robert E. Lee invaded Pennsylvania in 1863 and was possibly heading for Philadelphia in a huge arc to encircle Washington, D.C., the threat to the city grew.[8] One of the city's own, George Meade was the general whose men stopped the Confederates in the terrible battle of Gettysburg. The commotion in Philadelphia, the anguished worries before the battle and the relieved adulation of Meade after it, would have been difficult for even the most dedicated art student to ignore.

Eakins was in good company; it would not have done the shelves of our libraries or the walls of our museums a service if Henry James, Henry Adams, and Thomas Eakins had been slaughtered at Fredericksburg. (All three of these complicated brilliant men may have paid a psychological price for their escape, but, in the deep recipe for the making of the human mind, the number of tablespoons of war needed to permanently flavor a psyche is past knowing.)

Word of the terrible losses in General Grant's invasion of Virginia in the spring of 1864, culminating in the horror of Cold Harbor in June would have been enough to warn off a prudent man now in danger of being drafted into that army. On July 25 of that year, Eakins turned twenty. In August, with, one suspects, the encouragement of his father, Tom went to the recruiting office of Philadelphia's Fifth Ward and put down his twenty-five dollars as a bounty payment.[9] He provided what might induce someone else to go to war and ensured that he would not.

On September 22, 1866, the war over, Thomas Eakins sailed from New York to Paris to study art. His father, John Sartain, and Emily Sartain were there to see him off on the *Periere*. A long letter, mailed when he reached Paris, began, "Such is a mother's love, that the letter most acceptable to her will be as full of I's as one of [President] Johnson's speeches." And so it is. As they left the harbor on their swift boat, the "sun was pretty warm and we did not dine till half-past four. I got as far as the end of the soup, and prudently retired. I then lost all account of . . . everything else. I think it must be worse than cholera at least as far [as] sensations go." "One night my dreams were better. . . . I heard one of Fanny's sonatas from beginning to end; I do not think I missed a note and this I look upon as extraordinary, for if awake I could not have begun to remember it. Then I was eating ice-cream; then, I had been rowing with Max and I was drinking some cool beer . . . but while I was drinking some one put salt in it, and I was still forced to drink it." An attentive purser got him to swallow "a couple of mouthfuls of bread and some wine"; by then several days had mercifully passed. "By dinner time my appetite was as good as ever, and if my sickness was sudden, my recovery was no less so and now I am as well as ever in my life if not better."[10]

Eakins wrote vividly of the trip: "The ocean is different from what I expected. The waves are much larger. When people said mountains, I always thought of mole-hills. The general size is between the two. The wind except for two or three days has been east right against us." One day, he reports, the sea "was perfectly calm. One could not have wanted a better place to row." Then, a sudden storm came and, in minutes, it went from "hot almost to suffocation" to "almost freezing cold; . . . the officers came up on deck, and such a blowing of boatswains' whistles

and a giving of orders I have not heard since I started," a performance
Eakins thought excessive for the "small affair. . . . An hour afterwards the
stars were all shining."[11]

Tom was curious about his shipmates and opinionated in his accounts
of them. One "looks like an Irishman," is "dirty," and "has no just appreciation of the difference between his things and mine." Another, who
shared his grapes, "is the picture of a Philadelphia fireman . . . a rough"
who nonetheless was at home in French, Italian, Spanish, and German
and "read to me some of my Dante, not I think extremely well." "A
great savage eater and drinker," he reported to Eakins that his father had
been a "rebel" general "who owned 350 slaves [of whom] not one had
left the plantation, that they would work for whatever his father would
give them." Eakins seems not to have doubted the former slaves' docil-
ity, but he had no great opinion of the shipmate. The son goes "to Lyon
to study ten years," which Eakins judges will be the waste of a decade.[12]

There is also in their second-class cabin "an old negro in our cabin
going over to France to receive a medal for having saved a good many
cholera patients in Guadeloupe or some such place. He plays the fiddle."
Another passenger is a "young negro taking over wild animals to the
king of Italy; he was on his sixth voyage on that account." Eakins
explains, "He goes over the Alps with mule trains." Tom was happy
about his polyglot second cabin: "the first cabiners are nearly all Jews
and Americans." He closes, "I am scribbling in great haste for they will
soon put out my light"; they were about to reach Brest.[13]

The École des Beaux-Arts, Paris. (Photograph by Chuck LaChiusa)

IV

ÉCOLE DES BEAUX-ARTS

T
HE BOY FROM Philadelphia walked the streets of the city of all our fancies. Paris was Paris. If there was poverty and discontent, it was out of sight to Thomas Eakins. France was at peace and its capital a great city for walking, unless you found yourself in Baron Haussmann's way.[1] As prefect of the Seine, Georges-Eugène Haussmann had taken charge of Louis Napoleon's huge effort at urban renewal, the vast nineteenth-century demolition of whole stretches of old Paris in order to accommodate great boulevards and new buildings. There were those who found fault with the autocracy of the emperor, but such thinking was not of much interest to the remarkably apolitical, determined young artist from America. And if Louis Napoleon, in matters public, called for morality, few were listening. The capital was in its sensuous glory.

The energy in the air was unmatched, and Thomas Eakins breathed deeply. "The buildings of Paris are beautiful beyond description," he wrote to his mother. "Paris is a city of palaces. To beautify things the sun came out yesterday; today there has not been a cloud." The Philadelphian found the streets on the Left Bank more crooked than those in Boston, and they constantly changed their names. Everything in the city is different, he tells his mother: the "carriages, animals, dresses. . . . The quays of the Seine are always full of people . . . fishing." The Luxembourg Gardens were at their loveliest, and full of birds: "They flock by the thousands. . . . Any bird will come and feed out of your hand . . . it is fun . . . to get a crowd of tom-tits around you; . . . put a little piece of bread on your thumb and shoot it like a marble. . . . I have not yet seen a crumb fall to the ground." Nearby Tom spotted a carousel: "wooden horses that go round in a circle of about 30 ft. to the number of 10 or 12 . . . the smallest children are strapped tight so they can't fall off, and then the man in the middle turns the crank which moves the concern." Everything around him catches his eye: "Paris is full of soldiers. . . . They are dazzling, and you see them in every street. The most beautiful are the dragoons with their long swords and carbine. They mostly go at full gallop."[2]

As he closed this long letter to his mother, he betrays a bit of homesickness: he asks about his sisters' schooling and hope that they all "have been boating. Our Schuylkill is so beautiful at this season. I hope Poppy goes out regularly with Max. Has the opera come to Philadelphia yet? There are several here."[3] Throughout his life Eakins was devoted to opera, heard some of the nineteenth century's best, and knew them well.

In his savoring of the city, Eakins did not forget why he had come. He would be a painter. With that goal firmly in mind, he had arrived in Paris wearing his father's pat on the back and carrying a sheaf of letters of recommendation. As useful as these was his mastery of the French language. His goal was to gain a place in the holiest of holy of France's institutions for artists, the École des Beaux-Arts. Being foreign was a liability grudgingly offset by his fluent French. Never again was Eakins as adroit or as successful in arguing on his own behalf as he was in working his way through the labyrinth of French governmental bureaucracy.

Tom's aim was to secure a place in the school under the tutelage of its ranking painter-teacher, Jean-Léon Gérôme. He had several letters of introduction, made several attempts to find someone who would help him open the door, and was dispirited until he made use of his most valuable letter. It was written by John Sartain, a frequent visitor to Paris and well-known in the city's art circles. Sartain had recognized Tom's promise and said so explicitly in a letter directly to Albert Lenoir, secretary of the École. It worked. Calling on Lenoir after hearing repeatedly that all places in the school were taken, Eakins learned that one had suddenly opened.

Lenoir advised Eakins that he had only to be vouched for by John Bigelow, the American minister to France (as ambassadors were still known). Like Charles Francis Adams in Great Britain, Bigelow had been busy keeping his hosts from supporting the Confederacy; now, with the war over, he was a good deal more available than he had been. Nevertheless, a fawning flunky, whom Eakins found immensely irritating, tried to keep him from seeing the minister. Tom turned a deaf ear to the gentleman and eventually was admitted to Bigelow's office. There he not only persuaded the cordial minister to write a letter vouching for him, but also convinced Bigelow to include in his letter a request that Eakins' Philadelphia friend Earl Shinn, as well as another Pennsylvanian, Howard Roberts ("a rich disagreeable young man"), and two other American applicants who had failed in their attempt to gain admission, be allowed through the gate. Bigelow told Eakins that he "hoped I would make as good an artist as diplomat."[4]

Triumphantly, Eakins went back to Lenoir, who enrolled him, tentatively listing him as a student of Gérôme, dependent on the completion of the paperwork. Not wanting to wait on French bureaucracy, Eakins asked if he might go directly to the master, with whom he very much wanted to work, to gain his acquiescence. Again, Lenoir agreed and Eakins eagerly set off. Gérôme was painting from a model in his studio when Eakins arrived and, with a bit of shameless confidence, interrupted the great man to articulate how much he wanted to work with him. Gérôme, his considerable ego fed, was charmed; he hesitated just a moment, put down his brush, and wrote a letter to the director of the École, instructing that Eakins be assigned to him as a student.

Eakins thought this should settle the matter, but no. Imperial approval was also needed. At the emperor's vast suite of offices, he expected only

to have to show Lenoir's, Bigelow's, and Gérôme's letters to gain admit-
tance to the school. Lucien Crépon, a Parisian artist who had befriended
the Eakins family while living in Philadelphia, advised Tom to put all the
documentation in a large impressive envelope. Eakins reports that he
"accepted this amendment with rapture," stuck the little note inside,
addressed the envelope to "Mr. the Count of Nieuwerke [sic], superin-
tendent of the House of the Emperor & of the Fine Arts," and set off.
"What rows of soldiers & servants! Each one must know my business."
Feigning ignorance of French, Tom refused to yield the envelope to any
of them and eventually he was admitted to the anteroom of Count
Nieuwerkerke. Again, he was asked to give up his precious letters that
he suspected, no doubt accurately, would languish on some underling's
desk. So, when no one was looking, he pulled the letters out of the
envelope and put in his tiny calling card instead.[5]

In his office, the count looked at the card and sent back word that
since he hadn't met Eakins, he could not receive him, but would read a
petition. Eakins hurried home, worked over what he desperately hoped
would be winning prose, and returned the next day with the envelope
now full of letters for the minister. He was told to return the next afternoon for answer, which he did—only to be told, after a long wait, that
the minister had not had time to read it. So, he returned the next afternoon, this time with his copy of Dante. Finally, he was told that the
count had read Eakins' plea and turned the matter over to an underling.
Where was this man? Tom was given a slip of paper with a name on it,
which got him to another clerk, who gave him another slip with
another name—"if I'm ever king I vow to create the 'Order of the Little
Slip of Paper.'" After going from desk to desk, only to learn that the
eminent count's deputy, M. Tournois could only be seen on Tuesday or
Saturday at two in the afternoon, Eakins smiled and, laboriously, in his
fanciest French stated syllable by syllable, that he had seen the count
himself. Eventually he was admitted to M. Tournois's presence—who
proved amiable, acted as if the matter was routine, and sent Tom off with
the precious endorsement in the famous envelope.[6]

Proud of himself, Tom wrote to his father of his success and added that he had been told that it had taken one American a year to work his way through the maze while another had been waiting: "Roberts has been here a long time & he is very rich and his father sent him to enter the school." Now Tom Eakins could walk through the hallowed doors and gloat just a bit that his lobbying—and not money—had gotten Roberts, as well as the other Americans, admitted on his coattails.[7]

Tom Eakins proved, for once, a masterly storyteller in this long letter of October 26–27, 1866, but at its end the tone of self-confidence and humor suddenly shifts. He makes some strange observations about human character, he worries over having had to "descend to petty deceptions" in his quest for a place in the École, but thinks them justified since they were "practiced on a hateful set of little vermin, uneducated except in low cunning, who have in all their lives perverted what little minds they had, have not left one manly sentiment." This excessively sour observation comes just before he takes a telling look at himself. Tom reminds his father, "You have often accused me of being either in the garret or the cellar" and adds that the remark "had a fine application in Paris, . . . never were garrets so lofty or cellars so deep."[8] Benjamin Eakins was not in the business of being a therapist, but the image he applied to his son suggests bipolarity. Tom's swing in language from humorous and triumphant in his account of coping with the bureaucracy to his mean-spirited assessment of the clerks in the minister's office is suggestive of what Benjamin Eakins observed in his son. The wise father had spotted within his son traces of a condition that chased Eakins throughout his life.

When Eakins turned up at Gérôme's studio at the École for his first day, he noticed smirks on the porters' faces as one of them, with excessive solemnity, led him to the studio, introduced Eakins as a newcomer—and hastily slammed the door. The French students were lying in wait for the new boy. They crowded around him, giving a huge yell, and, to see what rise they could get out of him, mockingly called him "a pretty child." "How gentle. How graceful." They then, with a bribe in mind, set up a chorus of twenty francs. Eakins, not taking their bait, but getting what they were up to, waited until they quieted down

to ask to whom he had to give the francs. Now there was a discordant
chorus of "to me, to me," whereupon a large, heavily bearded man of
thirty (a tad over the top for boyish pranks) told his peers they were
"hogs" and, putting his face a nose length away from Eakins', made
bizarre funny faces. Eakins reported to his father that "I looked pleas-
antly on and neither laughed nor [appeared] angry. I tried to look
merely amused." When it came to language, he had them. Without
bothering to listen to his French, they mocked his "Musheers," accusing
him of being English. "My god no, gentlemen, I'm an American," Tom
replied. "(I feel sure that raised me a peg in their estimation.)" But he
had to put up with being called a "savage"—a Huron or an Algonquin
—and the assumption that he must be rich. There was some remarkable
confusion, possible only among the French, over his native tongue—
"some of them really did not know what was the language of
Americans"—one student asked him if it were German. When Eakins
replied, in German, his interrogator couldn't reply in kind. In all, he
emerged from the hazing ahead of the game. When things calmed
down, he made his escape, thanking them "for their kind attention."[9]

A little breathless from the encounter, Eakins went for advice to
Crépon. Tom explained the day's escapade; what should he do about the
twenty francs? With a shrug, Crépon told him to pay them and go along
with their "old custom" as best you can—and supplied Eakins with the
francs. In time, Tom philosophically wrote to his father that they were
an ill-mannered lot, taken together, but amiable one by one. "I will be
sorry if I ever have an enemy amongst them."[10]

That day Eakins had displayed his remarkable ability to be at ease in
a studio-classroom—even if, later, in other rooms, he was equally well-
known for his irascibility. Breaking the ice with the French students was
doubly fortunate when, under Eakins' wing, the next American student
appeared at the École. Harry Moore was deaf. He and Tom had been
students together at the academy. An uncle had taken the young Moore
to Gérôme and gained his allegiance, but getting along with fellow students in the studios of the École was another matter. To his wardrobe of
languages, Eakins quickly added sign language and became Moore's

"ears" in the studio. "I have no doubt my assuming the protection of Harry has in a measure protected me also," he reported home. "There is no one in the studio who speaks English and I'm glad of it."[11] As he signed, he instinctively mouthed the words to Moore, without worrying about what he was saying.

Moore wasn't the only American student in Eakins' debt. Earl Shinn, whose original application to the École had been rejected, went off hiking. He later wrote his family, "The fact is that while I was rambling in Brittany, young Tom Eakins was exerting himself, in the heat, investigating Directors and bothering Ministers, until he got the whole list of American applicants admitted. They had decided to exclude foreigners."[12] Now, thanks to a fellow foreigner, Shinn was also to study at the École.

There is a certain gravity in the language that Eakins used in his letter to his father. Once, describing the hazing that went on at the École, he told of "a disagreeable boy in our school who by want of every gentlemanly quality was disliked by all the school." One day, "on entering he was at once thrown & tied. . . . Then he was buried under the box we have to set casts on . . . & we sung the De Profundis & some other grand old church tunes of the dead." As if this weren't enough, "he was tied upside down or crucified as it is called & blindfolded . . . & they cut off the right side of his hair & the left side of his beard." Not surprisingly, once the officials of the École learned of the incident, they were not amused and the students were all suspended for a week. Eakins closed his lengthy account with a request of his father that "he will not waste any sympathy on the nasty little brat. I am not fond of injustice . . . & neither am I cruel. . . . I don't think he got half what he deserved." Yet you sense that Tom, protesting too much, was less than proud of the whole business and was confessing to his father, hoping for forgiveness.[13]

One evening, Eakins, along with Shinn and Billy Sartain, was a guest for dinner with Harry Moore, his mother, father, and recently widowed sister, who had accompanied Harry to Paris and set up housekeeping. A few weeks later, Shinn sent home a striking portrait of Eakins that suggests the paradox of awkwardness, single-mindedness, and charm that was characteristic of him. Recalling the evening at the Moores, Shinn wrote: "They fool with him; and treat him like a little child. . . . He is 21 [actually he was twenty-two], converses in Italian, French and German with the manners of a boy. Restricts his conversation pretty much to stories of the Schuylkill boating club." It was a different story when the two were alone: "I had him up in the room a fortnight since, —fancy a long evening in awkward silence, except fluttering of paper and scratching of pencils: my wrist ached after he was gone. He is an excellent fellow . . . and sharp as a razor. . . . Is the son of a writing master, tall, athletic, black hair and splendid eyes. Look out, young widow treating the dangerous young Adonis as a boy."[14]

V

LUXEMBOURG GARDEN

THOMAS EAKINS' PARIS address was a room in a tall slim house at 46, rue de Vaugirard. Across the street was Marie de Médicis's Palais de Luxembourg. The vast gloomy structure was backed by a magnificent garden, one of the nicest spots in Paris. Tom wrote home of walks alone on the gravel paths through the park. His street, one of the main routes into the city from the south, was crowded with wagons full of farm produce often slowed by herded animals being driven into market. Tom's house stood atop a hill at the foot of which was the École. He could get to his school by walking down past the famous old church of St. Suplice and gaining the busy Boulevard St. Germain. Ducking the traffic of carriages, he would cross at the Church of St.-Germain-des-Pres, choosing the rue Bonaparte to reach the École on his left.

The art world in Paris was at its greatest moment, the advent of impressionism, but Tom learned of it only in its refutation. He was to study with the man accepted as the ranking academic painter in Paris, but Jean-Léon Gérôme, like the rest of Paris, was blind to what was to

Luxembourg Gardens, Paris. (Library of Congress)

become the great impressionist school. Again and again, Tom cites his mentor's pronouncements on what great art was, to which list Eakins always appended Gérôme himself, giving him privilege of place. The teacher's appraisals did nothing to open Eakins' eyes to the world of Manet and Monet; Gérôme was notorious for his scorn of the newer painters, who were to leave him in the backwater.

What of Eakins' own curiosity? In 1865, in a major show, Édouard Manet exhibited his *Olympia*. The bold, naked young woman staring out at all of Paris was a sensation. The painting was probably not on public display during Eakins' time in Paris, but when he arrived in 1866, it was still the subject of controversy. Had he been eager to see it, he surely could have wangled an introduction to Manet and had a look in his studio. (Another Manet picture that Eakins might have been curious about was of the USS *Kearsarge* destroying the Confederate *Alabama* just off the French coast; it had taken a Frenchman to give us the finest rendering of an American Civil War battle.) Manet shared Eakins' fondness for the Spanish painters, and the work of the Frenchman and the American had a good deal in common. Both painted realistically observed people who intrigued them. But they were oblivious of each other. In 1866, Manet met Monet and

Cézanne—the forward-looking art community was getting stronger day by day, but Eakins was not part of it.

Perhaps it is just as well that he wasn't. As good as Eakins was at Manet's forte, figure painting, he might easily have been seduced into becoming an expatriate artist, rather than the quintessential American one that he was. There was in Eakins a private distancing from the kinds of excitement that absorbed the public. Tom's long, thorough letters home—particularly to his father, his sister Fanny, and Emily Sartain—tell us much about his work in the École with Gérôme and some of how he entertained himself in Paris. He describes trips through the Louvre and many evenings at the opera—*Martha, The Daughter of the Regiment*, and others—and at the theater, but not much more.

Eakins took advantage of his stay in Europe to go hiking with Billy Sartain and another old school friend, Will Crowell, in Switzerland in the summer of 1867 (they stopped at Strasbourg to see Tom and Billy's teacher Schussele). The following summer, when his father and his sister Margaret were in Europe, he followed them to Italy and saw the rich art on display in Rome, Genoa, and Florence. For Christmas 1868, through March 1869, Eakins was home in Philadelphia. His Paris training was not keeping his nose to the grindstone. But as he experienced a good stretch of Europe, he never lost his determination to be a painter.[1]

In March 1867, he reports, "Gérôme has at last told me I might get to painting & I commence Monday," a major step in his training.[2] A year and a half into his study in Paris, he wrote his father something of his view of painting: "The big artist does not sit down monkey like & copy a coal scuttle or an ugly old woman like some Dutch painters have done nor a dung pile, but keeps his eye on Nature & steal his tools." Then, as if he were a New England transcendentalist prepared to go where nature would take him, Eakins launched into a complex metaphor to explain his theory of painting. The painter, Tom tells his father, learns what nature does with light and color and form, and "appropriates them for his own use. Then he's got a canoe of his own smaller than Nature's but big enough for any purpose except to paint the midday sun which is not beautiful at all. . . . With this canoe he can sail parallel to Nature's sailing. He will soon be sailing only where he wants." But if "he ever thinks he can sail another fashion from Nature . . . he will capsize or stick in the mud."[3]

Eakins' windy metaphor continues and finally beaches itself. But it suggests his determination to both be true to nature, and to say something "big." This sense of working in relation to nature is not unlike that of Eakins' impressionist contemporaries, who would explore the natural world and use the river Seine in their paintings. Eakins would wait until he was back to the Schuylkill to do so.

What else in the world's most seductive city attracted him? What were his experiences outside the boundary of domesticated letters home? Eakins could not have escaped the vibrant café life of Paris with all of its highly charged talk of politics, the arts, and gossip—always with the rich undercurrent of sexuality. If, as Shinn advised, the young female in the Moore family had an Adonis in her sights, there must also have been a glance or two on Paris streets from male eyes. Where did those famously penetrating eyes of Eakins rest? Athletics were far from a trivial dimension in Eakins' makeup. With his equally able and remarkably companionable father, he had been swimming for years. Of the many sports that interested him, swimming was most readily available in Paris, and he wasn't long in making his way into the Seine. (Foul the river was;

determined swimmers kept their noses above water.) When Benjamin Eakins visited his son, he too braved it. Stretches along the Seine were known as territories for men seeking male sex. The sight of Eakins' swimmer's body emerging from the water would not have gone unnoticed. How did he respond?

Homosexuality. That word, despite our somewhat self-righteous liberality, still sprinkles itching powder over any discussion of Eakins. Having sexual relations with men, as Eakins may well have, led triumphant champions in the gay world to claim Eakins as a brother. Traditionalists hold that Eakins either wasn't gay or never succumbed to temptation—or that it doesn't matter. But, it does matter; sexuality is, of course, part of the whole human, an essential part. To ignore that dimension of Eakins' life would be to have only a partial person in view. To view it as the single important factor in his life does the same disservice.

There have been scores of speculations about the nature and extent of Eakins' attraction to men, and little doubt that it existed. To probe for an explanation of its cause is futile. What should be asked instead is how it factors into the whole of Eakins' life and art. Part of the problem lies in terminology. The word "homosexuality" hadn't been invented when Eakins was a young man; homosexual love, of course, had long existed. The noun and all of its synonyms, ancient and contemporary, sound like a malignant growth. They obscure the constant benign human element of desire that was as active, if not more so, in the middle of the nineteenth century as at any other time. If the society of the time frowned on same-sex desire, it did so with a less lethal glower than it wore at the century's end. To quote a refreshing metaphor of Graham Robb's, "if homosexuals were under a cloud in the nineteenth century, it seldom rained."[4]

It is likely that some of Eakins' Parisian friends, most of them fellow art students, were homosexual. Certainly they were a lively bunch. He saw them in the café world, and in their homes as well. Through a fellow student of Gérôme's, Germain Bonheur, he met the famous Rosa Bonheur, Germain's half sister. Ten years earlier, she had painted her vast astonishing *Horse Fair*. Admired in England by Queen Victoria and in

France by Louis Napoleon and his empress, Eugénie (and bought by A. T. Stewart for his New York department store), *Horse Fair* made Bonheur renowned and invited the scorn (and envy) of far greater painters—though no one could challenge her mastery of her animal subjects. A minor measure of Bonheur's fame was her election as an honorary foreign fellow of the Pennsylvania Academy of the Fine Arts, a fact she cannot have missed mentioning to Eakins.[5]

Bonheur was the eccentric celebrity of the day, to the dismay of painters of a very different artistic vision. Cézanne's response to her vast hyperrealistic scene of oxen teams, *Tilling in Nivernais*, was stunning. "Yes," he said, "it is horribly like the real thing." Her way of life was like none other. Bonheur had left her large ornate Paris studios on rue de l'Ouest and moved a few blocks to the rue d'Assas, where she had another, even more grand atelier, stables with still more animals, and a home that she shared with her lover, Nathalie Micas. Her menagerie included local barnyard animals—Percheron horses and hulking bulls, pigs and chickens, as well as yaks, gazelles, and an eagle. Bonheur held one of only a handful of permits that allowed a woman to wear men's clothing on the streets of Paris. A famous photograph of Bonheur cuddled up on the ground with a lion cub, reveals a woman perfectly open about her lesbian relationship with Micas, whom she adored. Rosa Bonheur kept fashionable Paris in gossip for decades.[6]

A feminist who scorned the idea of male superiority, Bonheur once, in front of her female friends, chastised a gardener who ruined a fine specimen by cutting its root: "Isn't that a beautiful example of male intelligence?" As far as hetorosexual relations, a male friend recollected, "After my marriage, when RB was riding out with me, but this time in a lady's dress, we happened to meet a gentleman friend of mine." The friend remarked that the newlywed's wife, seeing the two riding together, might not approve. Bonheur replied that the lady needn't worry: "If only you knew how little I care for your sex, you wouldn't get such queer ideas into your head. The fact is in the way of males, I like only the bulls I paint."[7]

By 1868, Eakins had become acquainted with the Bonheur family and moved to a studio on what had been their street, rue l'Ouest. He was no longer working at the École on a regular basis, reporting instead to Gérôme's studio for criticism. He reported in a letter he wrote home to his sister Fanny, "Once or twice a week in the evenings I go to the Bonheurs. They let me come into the sitting room, we drink cider. The old lady & daughter the painter knit and scold their big brothers for not putting on a collar or a clean one. They smoke & nurse the cat and if a fellow don't want to talk or don't feel like it he sits and looks into the fire & feels just as comfortable as he can knowing that he can't go to bed without turning out into the cold again."[8] (It was February.)

All this quiet domesticity somewhat belies the legendary sophistication that Bonheur's salon claimed. Mlle. Bonheur was still making a great deal out of a visit from Emperess Eugénie some three years before Thomas Eakins was received. (Oddly, Eakins seems unclear just who was there on those evenings.) On another occasion Eakins and his friend Billy Sartain were invited for dinner at the Bonheurs. A fellow guest was a Bonheur cousin said to be interested in mechanical things. Eakins, eager to show the cousin an example of how "America beats the world in machinery," produced his Smith & Wesson revolver whereupon, Rosa reached in her pocket "and pulled out one of the same make." Sartain hadn't thought there was even one such gun in Paris. Which of the two owners was the more unlikely is debatable, but that evening at a Paris dinner table the Wild West was present, thanks to a young man from a normally mild Philadelphia and to an older woman in an exceedingly outré Paris.[9]

Bonheur opened Eakins' eyes to a far wilder, wackier world than he had ever known, one with a much more open attitude toward sex. There were, of course, plenty of Frenchmen Eakins' age who were no more hedonistic than good American boys were expected to be, but in Paris was a world that mocked such expectations. Had Eakins wanted to move out of his middle-class outlook entirely and enter fully into a gay world, he certainly could have done so in Paris. There were streets and bars in which men interested in other men could congregate, and Eakins could hardly have avoided the glances of men beckoning him toward that life. The same was true, if to a lesser extent, in Philadelphia, but Eakins was not a stranger there. Had his homosexual activities been reported, they almost certainly would have cut him off from friends and from the company of those in the sciences. There were many dimensions to Eakins' life that seem incompatible with conventional masculinity.

There were choices to be made. On a trip in 1868, Emily Sartain, an artist like her father and brother, one who had much in common with Tom, spent a good deal of time with him in the city. Later that summer, Emily wrote Tom a letter from Geneva, where she had gone to escape Paris: "I do not like the place, never did—now less than ever." They had parted after a difficult evening and their relationship was strained by his not coming to the railroad station to see her off. In the letter, Emily chided Eakins for speaking of not going with his sister and father on their trip through Europe: "Are your reasons for refusal strong enough to justify . . . spoiling their pleasure? And besides I think you need a change. . . . If you go away for a while from that hateful city of Paris, and be with your relatives in new scenes, the reviving of old associations and the forming of new ones, would restore your right judgmement [sic]—which I am afraid you have almost lost."[10]

What was it that was so troubling to Eakins' old family friend, a woman who may have thought of becoming a fiancée? She makes no reference to, for example, too much drinking or any other such transgression; neither does she sound as if she is jealous. There is something else: "When you left home and people talked of the temptations of the great city you were going to, I smiled at their fears. I thought of your singleness and purity of heart, and believed too that the warm love you had for me would be a safeguard to you, if any were needed. To my sorrow after only two years of absence I find you laughing at things you should censure, excusing your companions for their vices, and even joining with them, making yourself like them."[11]

That night, according to her letter, Emily cried herself to sleep. She reminded Eakins that he had refused to make the promise she had required of him. To her dismay, he had said a "necessity" might arise that would make him break it and it seemed to her that he must "have fan-cied" such a necessity. "You are ill, bodily and mentally. It would be bet-ter to give up the profession that you have chosen since your head is not strong enough to stand it, than that you should be ruined, body and soul. Come home," she implored, "and go to work at something else, rather than lose your power of distinguishing right from wrong."[12]

She insists she has "not lost faith" in him. "You need only go away a while from your vicious companions, freshen your mind and body, and you will go back to your work stronger and better, and I hope a better man." She says of her candid letter, "I have yielded a great deal to you, have I not? Yield this much to me—Go with your father and sister, resolve to get over your weakness, to look at things from a sound American, *home* point of view, to be a man." Emily was as close as a Philadelphia lady of 1868 could be to saying that Eakins was becoming homosexual. "Am I offending you?" she queried after preaching what cannot have been an easy sermon to deliver—or receive.[13]

Eakins did not reply at once to Emily—not until she had written again from Interlaken (the letter is lost). But reply he did, making light of the matter. He held no resentment; their friendship lasted. Ironically Emily would later come to see herself as an artist, rather than a wife and mother. In the letter he finally wrote, Tom blamed a model's schedule and helping his landlord move for his delay. With his thoughts running ahead of his syntax, he wrote: "I was touched deep by your loving inter-est in me and was going to try [to] laugh you out of your ridiculous fears for me who had already withstood through love a temptation that"—here he strikes out "belittles"—"makes St. Anthony"—then he strikes "a fool"—"along side of me." He claims that she is wrong in her assessment of his judgment, which, he claims, is based on "my perfect knowledge of my own Paris life. . . ." As he was to do for a lifetime, he was defending his powerful sense that he alone knew himself, and, Eakins continued, "I defend my vicious companions as you were pleased to call my friends whom you had never seen & I love."[14]

Is this evidence of Eakins' homosexuality? No. As Graham Robb noted in *Strangers*, his study of nineteenth-century homosexuality,

". . . a plague of euphemisms wiped out the traces of homosexual love."[15] Indeed, it could be argued that the lack of evidence *is* the evidence. Neither men nor women were apt to document their sexual actions, but there is much in the Eakins story to suggest that his sexual attraction was to men rather than women. This can be taken into account without either sounding the trumpet of celebrators of gay love, or protesting (too much) that he was not gay.

Tom's declaration to Emily is a sensitive and firm declaration of independence, but it was Emily's advice that prevailed, to the great advantage of American art, and at great cost to Eakins. Whoever were those "friends whom you have never seen & I love," he soon left them and Paris to return to Philadelphia. One perhaps-happy ending would have been for Tom and Emily, so deeply concerned about each other, to have a Philadelphia wedding, something for which more than a few of their families and friends had hoped.

That was not to be. The emotional exchange in Paris did not create a permanent rift between the two. Instead, Emily's frankness became the base of their lifelong friendship. There was never a wedding for Emily Sartain; Tom Eakins helped her as she carved out a single woman's career for herself as a well-regarded administrator of a strong art school for women. She had understood the core of Eakins' emotional life and perhaps this, in time, helped her grasp her own.[16]

Prado Museum, Madrid. (Library of Congress)

VI

SPAIN

"I must decide for myself . . ."

S PAIN, NOT FRANCE, held the key to Eakins' greatest paintings. The Louvre, thanks to the Napoleons, had a scattering of canvases from Spain, but not the best. In our day, with the constant borrowing of works from the world's greatest museums by their counterparts around the globe, in addition to the overflow of photographic images, good and bad, it is hard to remember that in Eakins' day it was only by traveling to the originals, or, poor second, by relying on black-and-white engravings, that unfamiliar paintings could be seen. Eakins' loyalty to Gérôme never wavered, but in the spring of 1869 he began working on his own on what was to be his greatest strength as an artist. He began to "paint heads."

Eakins began studying in the Montmartre studio of Léon Bonnat, a portrait painter, whom he regarded as Paris's finest. Bonnat came from Bayonne in southwestern France, near the Pyrenees and Spain, and gave Eakins a quiet word of exactly the right advice: go to Spain, or rather to the Prado, and study the work of Velázquez, admitting that he himself "was raised on the cult of Velázquez."[1]

A quest for Velázquez or no, it was weather that made Eakins take the trip. If April in Paris is heaven, in November it is not. In had been raining for two weeks straight, turning the city, so subtly colored when flooded with sun in the spring, into a gray dreariness all its own. Eakins' room was damp and uncomfortable and his woodstove inadequate. He developed a bad cold and his cough worried him. In the nineteenth century, tuberculosis was always a fear. Billy Sartain, who was also working in Bonnat's studio, had been to Spain, loved it, and urged the trip on his friend. Spain promised sun and warmth.

On the evening of November 29, 1869, "in a pouring rain, of course,"[2] Tom Eakins set out by train. A clutch of his friends came to see him off. It was still raining as the train left France to climb the Pyrenees; it came down out of snow-covered mountains into a beautiful sunlit Spain and Eakins was at once in love. Late fall in Madrid was chilly, but he found people-watching wonderful, attended Catholic mass in this very Catholic country, and set off for the Prado. The dour late-eighteenth-century building looked a bit old-fashioned and, on its exterior, not very welcoming; but once inside, Eakins defied the gloom of the endless rooms and made straight for the brilliance of the museum's treasures. He knew what he wanted to see, but wasn't prepared for the munificence of the collections. The museum owned forty-five Murillos; their Zurbarán *Crucificado*, echoed later in Eakins' own *Crucifixion*, had no figure other than the dead Christ in the stark painting. And then there were the faces. They were what truly engaged Eakins. It was the face of Zurbarán's St. Francis peering out from under the hood of his cloak that was striking. Eakins saw that, in Ribera's religious scenes, the faces, as in *Santiago el Mayor* and *San Pedro*, are portraits in themselves.

If something of these remarkable Spanish paintings remained in Eakins' head and moved to his canvases, the artist whose work spoke most strongly to him was Diego Velázquez. Many of his sixty works in the museum were portraits, each rich in enigmatic personality. The best of Eakins' work would one day approach them. Something wonderful and new lay before him in the Prado. Nothing in Gérôme's work, nor much in the Louvre, could approach these paintings. The tourist in the

Prado learned what years of earlier study in Philadelphia and Paris had not taught him.

Eakins had taken the classic route for an aspiring artist by moving to Paris, entering the École, and working with an established master. The strict training in technique under Gérôme's tutelage would be apparent in all Eakins' work and he was loyal to the master for a lifetime, but luckily Eakins' subjects were not to be at all like the exotic themes of Gérôme. The florid, brilliantly colored, sharply realistic canvases of the fashionable French painter's mythical nudes, his historical scenes, and his imagining of the exotic East were not to influence any Eakins canvas. We are spared any reprise of Gérôme's *We Who Are About to Die, Salute You* in which the gladiator speaks to the emperor as he enters the Colosseum. Worse still is his *The Nymph and Eros*, a glaring painting of a naked young boy, his backside staring at us as he faces a row of oriental potentates and retainers sitting on cushions and leering at him as he fondles a huge snake.[3]

It wasn't until he reached Spain that Eakins began to find his unique way. The Louvre had always disappointed him. Of the Prado he wrote, "O what a satisfaction it gave me to see the good Spanish work, so good, so strong, so reasonable, so free from every affectation. It stands out like nature itself. . . . It has given me more courage than anything else ever could."[4]

Eakins made notes (in French) as he walked through the galleries. He is struck by the "very beautiful color" in a Castiglione, notes the cracked condition of a Velázquez, sees a similarity in the way Ribera and Rembrandt worked. His notes reflect a highly personal eye. Of Goya's sketches (almost certainly those for the finished *Family of Carlos IV*, the famous picture of the king, his strikingly ugly queen, and the children of the royal family) he wrote that he "never saw more character in children's heads than his studies for a large family portrait." There were six children's faces, from an infant in arms to the teenage future king Ferdinand VII, in the finished painting. (Eakins himself was to do wonderful work with tiny children, but they typically were shown with their faces turned to their playthings.) Equally sharply, he noted subtle shifts in the stance of the royal family that told him that Goya must have changed positions as he painted. Eakins thought it "abominable stiff commonplace work."[5] (The celebrated canvas may still be hanging today on the same wall as it did in 1869—the place seems changeless. The painting is a tour de force of royal portraiture; Eakins was right that the not very promising family is indeed stiff, but stiffness may have been what Goya sought to convey.) Characteristically, Eakins, so resolutely uninterested in social matters, makes no mention of Goya's even greater works, *Los Desastres de la Guerra*, his unyielding multicanvas depiction of the horror of war, and his nightmarish figure of *Saturn Devouring His Son*.

Without a comment, Eakins was drawn, not to work of his own century, but to that of the seventeenth. It was as he stood in front of a Velázquez that Eakins made the most significant entry in his diary. The American tourist had, as two fellow artists have noted "a moment of epiphany for a young artist." He wrote, "I must decide for myself never to paint in the manner of the master [his term for Gérôme]." (Then, giving scant credit where he thought credit due, he added: "One can scarcely hope to be stronger than [Gérôme, but] he is far from painters like the Riberas and Velasquezes[.] Still he is stronger than some dabbler.")[6]

The American had declared his independence.

After Madrid, Eakins took the train to Seville, the ancient city in southwest Spain. There he met up with Harry Moore, his friend from Paris. Shortly afterward, Billy Sartain, also escaping from the rain of Paris, joined them.[7] Tom and Billy shared a corner room looking out on a crossroads of the city and onto the hotel's courtyard, which was filled with fragrant orange and lemon trees. (They were served vast breakfasts in their room and a rich array of tapas in the afternoon, all, Billy reported, for $1.50 a day, plus a good tip.) Settling in, Eakins hired a tutor and soon added his seventh language, "I speak Spanish enough every day to kill or deafen a Spaniard if my whole conversation could be addressed to one person."[8]

He and Harry walked the streets talking in animated sign language. Moore, Eakins told his father, "notices things, more than ordinary people. . . . He can see farther out of the corner of his eye than anyone I ever knew, & he sees everywhere gentlemen repressing the curiosity of the little children at our queer motions." In return, the sight of unusual people caught the Americans' attention. The three young men drank up the city—the gypsies, street dancers, dancers in the theaters, and, in true Sevillian style, the bullfights in the great yellow walled arena that *Carmen* made famous.[9]

It was the Requeña family of street dancers and musicians who particularly caught Eakins' eye and provided a breakthrough experience for him. At last, he set out to use his oils; the result was the first completed canvas of his career. Typical of the way he was to work all his life, Eakins threw himself with total commitment into the job of painting a child dancing, with her family playing for her. It is worth quoting at length from a letter to his father to get a sense of Eakins at work: "I have been lately working very hard & often in much trouble. . . . Sometimes I am at work at 6 o'clock & except to take my two meals I work on till 6 at night & then eat my dinner, I don't feel like doing anything at all but going to bed. If all the work I have put on my picture could have been straight work [his usual black-and-white drawings] I could have had a hundred pictures at least, but I had to change and bother, paint in & out. Picture making is new to me, there is the sun & gay colors & & a hundred things you never see in a studio light & ever so many botherations that no one out of the trade could ever guess at. I hope to soon be over the worst part."[10] Receiving this letter, Benjamin could see that he had a true painter on his hands.

Thomas knew it too. In January 1870 he wrote to his father, "My student life is over now & my regular work commenced."[11] Their landlord had turned over the flat roof of the hotel to Eakins. Out in the sunlight, so different from the light in the vast studios of the École des Beaux-Arts, he had to struggle with the unremitting glare of the brilliant Seville sun. (Back in the United States, he sketched outdoors scenes and painted back in his studio.) He was delighted with his models and talked of doing a gypsy and a bullfighter. If he did such pictures, he left them behind when he left Spain.

Concentration on his painting only increased Tom's appetite for getting out on horseback into the hills around Seville. He often led Harry Moore and Billy Sartain on forty-mile rides out from the city. The Requeña picture done, they set off in the late spring on a nine-day pack trip into the Andalusian mountains. Crossing the river they rode south through the valley, up into the plains and finally climbed into the mountains that are so frequent in Spain. It took three days to arrive at "the remote old city of Ronda," situated on a rocky crag. (Ronda had been one of the last places to fall to Ferdinand and Isabella's ruthless routing of the Moors who had lived in Andalusia for centuries.) "Part of the way over mountains where there were no roads—only occasional tracks made [by previous travelers]. . . . It was thus for long stretches over hills & mountainsides, a vast solitary waste," wrote Sartain. "At night we would sleep in the inns, consisting of one long cobblestone paved room—at the further end our horses and mules & our baggage, nearer part devoted to cooking and eating." They slept on mattresses only an inch thick "through which the stones were plainly felt." The trip was strenuous, but not overly so. With Billy and particularly Harry in the company, nothing was left to frugality; a groom followed them with mules and their luggage.[12]

The three left Seville at the end of May for Madrid and another look at the Prado before returning to a nervous Paris, deeply uneasy in the aftermath of the defeat in the Franco-Prussian War. The Commune was established that fall, only to be ruthlessly destroyed by right-wing opponents. Eakins, with his almost uncanny ability to miss history, sailed for home in June. He was back in Philadelphia for the Fourth of July.[13]

John Biglin in a Single Scull, 1873–74. (Yale University Art Gallery)
See color plate 3.

VII

PHILADELPHIA

T OM WAS BACK in Philadelphia for good. The trip to Europe had been an awakening experience, but a singular one. Those years had been rich ones, but the resulting treasure went into an attic trunk, which was never opened again. Back downstairs, Eakins was immediately engaged in the intensity of family life at a particularly dark time. His mother, at fifty, was desperately unwell. Caroline Eakins, who had not made the trip to Europe with her husband and daughter Margaret in 1868, was by 1870 virtually housebound. There is nothing in the correspondence to suggest that Tom was summoned home to comfort his mother, but once back, that demand was inescapable. If the house at 1729 Mt. Vernon Street had for twenty years provided Caroline with a sense of security, it now had become a place of dread. At forty-five, her third pregnancy with Caddy may have been difficult. There is no evidence of what that experience brought to the mother. This period is in fact a strange blank in the family history. We get only a fleeting sense of the demons that terrified Caroline. As the months wore on she could not bear to be alone.

When Caroline Eakins died on June 4, 1872, the death certificate cited "exhaustion from mania," a phrase that only hints at the mother's anguish, the terrible lurching around the house, the frantic swirling of terror in a body that finally gave way. Neither Tom nor his father or sisters left any record of these grim days, but they must have left their mark on the helpless family. In the many photographs, there are signs that Thomas Eakins had seen mental illness and was not immune to it; his erratic response to events and people suggests that Eakins was a fellow sufferer from a lesser, but real, case of depression.

For Caroline Eakins there was a burial in Philadelphia's proper Woodlands Cemetery. For her son, a sense of pressure; the heavier the weight of his mother's condition and her death, the greater the need to work. With only one painting behind him, the street dancers in Seville, it was time to take on America. Out came his oils. In his first five years back in town, Eakins turned out a remarkable body of work. Some of the loveliest paintings were related to the demands that kept him at home, the closed-in scene of these first paintings. His sister Caddy at six sits on the handsomely carpeted floor writing on her slate while an older sister, at the piano, looks down at her. In a later interior picture, a close family friend, Elizabeth Crowell (Will's sister), also sits at the piano, that emblem of a correct American household, on which an almost legible piece of sheet music is being played. There is a resolutely unglamorous picture of his favorite sister, Margaret, almost sullen in an unflattering skating costume, ready for a family outing on the ice. All of this he portrayed in the darkened parlor of 1729 Mt. Vernon Street. The house, well lit upstairs where Tom had his studio, was grieving. The paintings are familial; handsome rather than joyous.

Once outdoors, Tom was a true Philadelphian. Rowing was his favorite sport; the row of boathouses where he kept his scull was within walking distance. Here he had his hands on a pair of oars. His grip was strong and steady. The blades hover above the water cleanly on the return. The slim wood shell skims above the surface as his legs drive and his back straightens. The work is pleasurable and, to the observer, effortless. Again, his wrists curl and drop as he lifts his blades out cleanly at

Home Scene, 1871. (Brooklyn Museum of Art)
See color plate 4.

the finish of his stroke; he feathers them with a flick of the wrist and continues the steady, gliding return. The twin blades balance the boat like an acrobat's bar, only to dip again suddenly into the water at the catch. Catch, drive, glide, his bulky body sends the fragile shell skimming, an arrow on the Schuylkill's quiet surface.

Thomas Eakins was out on the Schuylkill River, which flows through

Philadelphia, its surface the scene of the city's characteristic sport—sculling in slim, beautiful boats. In one of his best-known paintings, *Max Schmitt in a Single Scull*, he paints himself in his own scull, but far to the rear of the canvas. He is looking down toward his friend Max Schmitt, the champion sculler, who in turn looks back at us, presenting a striking portrait of the lean athlete. In the painting, an arched bridge of heavy stones carries the railroad into the city, as if to tie the painter to his time and his work. Save for the stay in Europe, his life was lived, his work done, here in Philadelphia—with few escapes into New Jersey and the Pennsylvania countryside. Eakins portrayed an America inhabited by people he knew and by those his nineteenth-century curiosity drew him to.

Eakins captured to perfection the educated middle class Philadelphia of craftsmen like his upholsterer father-in-law and music teachers. But there was another Philadelphia that Eakins seems to have known not at all. Working-class Americans, black and white, and European immigrants lay outside his line of vision. So too did factory Philadelphia. At the time of his birth, Philadelphia was the most industrialized city in the country.[1] Once the nation's capital, Philadelphia was no longer the country's political center; its power as the financial center had been lost to New York when Andrew Jackson killed Nicholas Biddle's central Bank of the United States. But Philadelphians did not yet feel their city slipping behind. Across the river in Camden they were busy making the Campbell's soup that later enriched the Dorrance family in the first half of the twentieth century, Andy Warhol in its second. The Baldwin Locomotive Works, producing the immense, powerful engines that drove the nation's railroads, was only one of forty major Philadelphia factories.

As a teenager Tom had been comfortable in the snug seat he confidently filled in a single scull. But it was not to make him content. Thomas Eakins was one of the nineteenth century's remarkable seekers. He was, in fact, the last of them. The others, save the poet Walt Whitman, were silent by the time he did much of his greatest work. And, unlike Thoreau or Emerson, Eakins' way of telling us what was America—what it might become—was as a painter rather than as a writer. Eakins and the writers before him knew the world they lived in had never been

Rail Shooting, on the Delaware (Will Shuster and Blackman Going Shooting for Rail).
(Yale University Art Gallery)
See color plate 5.

idyllic, and they had not expected it to be, yet they yearned for something that reached beyond comfort and progress.

Eakins was an alarmingly American, or, indeed, Philadelphian, painter of the city's upper-middle class, better described as its professional class. In his pictures, workingmen were usually observed by well-dressed townspeople watching their meticulous work, as in one version of *Shad Fishing at Gloucester on the Delaware River* and in *Mending the Net.* There is also a strange group of paintings that represent Eakins' imaginings of olden days, but the figures here are simply the usual crowd playing dress up. Even his sole *Crucifixion* was domesticated.

In a painting of a favorite sport, Eakins was an inch away from a strong statement on race. In the 1876 picture *Will Shuster and Blackman Going Shooting for Rail*, we are once again out in the reeds after rail— this time with a difference. Will Shuster, white, a family friend, stands in the bow of a boat, his gun cocked. In the stern a black man skillfully

Eakins at about age twenty-four.
Photograph by Frederick
Gutekunst. (The Pennsylvania
Academy of the Fine Arts)

poles the small craft, ensuring that the boat remains steady when Shuster shoots. Shuster is depicted as a rather slight, unimpressive figure, wearing a silly hat and a bright red shirt. The poler, nameless, is taller than Shuster. The sleeve of his shirt is rolled over his muscular bicep. He, rather than Shuster, is the central figure in the painting. Even his hat makes more sense than does Shuster's and his clearly delineated expression is that of intense concentration as he watches his charge. Eakins can be accused of being one of many American artists who largely excluded black subjects, gave them only a face in the crowd; here, however, almost without realizing what he has accomplished, he has not only included a black subject, but made him the picture's center. And then insulted him by denying him a name.[2]

It was as if Eakins had taken Emily Sartain's advice. She had extolled him to be her kind of American, with the full panoply of his European

Starting Out After Rail, 1874. (Museum of Fine Arts, Boston)
See color plate 6.

adventures resolutely behind him. In all of Eakins' pictures—most famously, his pictures of rowers—his brush portrayed the vibrant outdoors, but his method was that of an engineer at his drafting table, rather than that of the man who struggled with the glare of the sun on a hotel rooftop in Seville. Having precisely measured a shell down to the inch, he reproduced with mathematical precision, lines on the canvas for *The Biglin Brothers Turning the Stake-Boat*, his study of champions in a two-man shell competing in Philadelphia. Exhaustive in his preparation, Eakins made tiny dolls, complete with authentic head rags, that he placed in a model of the boat and bent to the task of sculling. With seeming effortlessness, he painted the great picture as if he had held his brush at the exact moment of the race.

Gloucester City, New Jersey, downriver from Philadelphia, was a favorite spot for outings and the scene of wonderful sailing pictures: *Sailboats Racing on the Delaware*, men pressing in a light breeze, and *Starting Out after Rail*, a gaff-rigged sail catching the wind as one of Eakins' friends bends to the tiller and rudder while the boat swiftly carries him and his passenger out over dappled water. Back in the city, Eakins went to a ball game and painted *Baseball Players Practicing*, with a scattering of fans in the stands watching a batter awaiting a pitch. These are as comforting as any paintings in America, and as American. There is nothing amatory in Eakins' gaze. As the sports pages are compared with page one of our newspapers, we find ourselves here in a world of harmless strife and momentarily out of reach of a world of anguish.

In 1875 came the remarkable leap to what Eakins always considered his most important painting; some critics call *The Gross Clinic* America's greatest painting. To the artist, never was it bested in the remaining forty years of his life, in which he pursued his deep interest in science. Eakins had met Samuel Gross, perhaps the city's finest surgeon, in the mid-1860s. Eakins was studying anatomy and Gross was coming to the Pennsylvania Academy of the Fine Arts to draw. Now he undertook a subject he thought more important than his sporting pictures. Eakins had the story of an operation to tell in all its fierce intensity.

We are in an operating theater of a teaching hospital. The auditorium is filled with students, most, if not all, attentive to the demonstration of surgery at work. (In Alfred Hitchcock fashion, Eakins himself is among them.) The patient's left buttock and thigh are bared as one surgeon, scalpel in hand, probes the incision with tools held by two assistants, one of them a young student. A third man holds the toweled anesthetic to the patient's face. A female figure, black-clad, veiled, and horrified, sits next to the operating table. Conventionally, she is said to be the mother

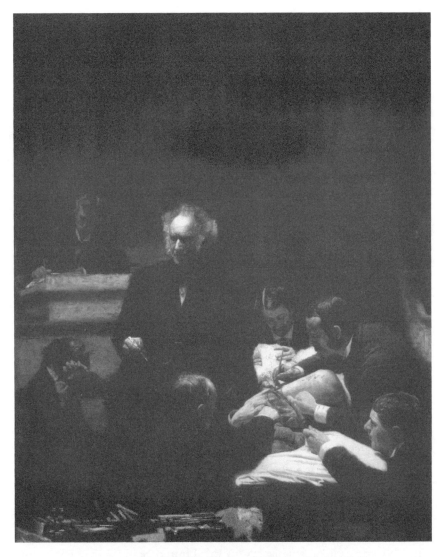

The Gross Clinic, 1875. (Thomas Jefferson University)
See color plate 7.

of the owner of the defective thigh, for lack of any sensible way of explaining why she is there.[3]

A professionally detached clerk keeps record of the surgery at a desk nearby. And dominating it all is Gross himself, his forehead in a light as intense as that on the flesh of the patient. The opposite of godlike, Gross is a human in command of the business of saving a life. The great surgeon

is standing to one side, a bloody scalpel in hand. It, like the open incision is scarlet. Other than two towels, there is not a speck of the hospital white so present in Eakins' other, later surgery painting. At the time,
surgical teams still wore business suits.

A camera could not have caught the whole of the story with the
drama Eakins portrayed. Squeamish viewers thought *The Gross Clinic* far
too vivid, even disgustingly candid; that bloody scalpel in the eminent
man's hand was too much for genteel eyes. It was not what gallery-goers
expected of art: there could be gore in the romps of gods or the torture
of saints in Renaissance masterpieces, but not in Philadelphia. If Eakins
did not anticipate the virulence of this reaction, he may not have found
it entirely dismaying. There is a harsh reality to an operation, and people should see it.

The United States was about to celebrate its one hundredth birthday
with a with a party in Philadelphia, with the Centennial Exposition in
Fairmount Park. In 1776, Philadelphia had been the birthplace of the
nation, with the signing of the Declaration of Independence, which said
no to monarchy. A century later, it might as well have been a thousand
years old—President Ulysses S. Grant was to open the celebrations with
an emperor in tow, Dom Pedro II of Brazil.[4]

The Declaration of Independence promised us a world in which all
men are created equal, but the centerpiece of the Centennial Exposition
was not a glass case displaying that document or even a battle-torn flag
from the American Revolution. Grant, for his part, could take credit for
having put us one step toward Jefferson's promise of equality by winning the war that ended slavery in the United States. His guest, however, governed the largest slaveholding nation on the globe.

The opening ceremony had the two heads of state paying homage to
what could be said to be the apogee of the age of industry: the Corliss,
engine. This wonder of the era was on display as the focus of the whole
fair. The giant pair of pistons, seven hundred tons in weight had been
hauled by rail freight from Rhode Island to power the exposition's endless array of equipment in Machinery Hall.

Almost everything on display was a Gloria to the manufacturing might of the age. On the cover of a catalogue of the great fair published by the popular *Frank Leslie's Illustrated Weekly*, America is surrounded by Europa, a kneeling American Indian, an adoring Asian, and a bare-breasted African. The whole illustration is done in the style of the elaborate engraving on the thousands upon thousands of shares of stock in mighty manufacturing corporations. Their wares and often the machinery that produced them were on display. Surely the most ominous of this output was one of Krupp's great cannon, terrifying to behold.

"All men are created equal" was acknowledged only by a mediocre statue of an almost naked black man, his shorn shackle at his feet. In the catalogue, an immaculately dressed black woman shows the statue to her equally properly dressed children. No sharecroppers they.

The display of *The Gross Clinic* was expected to launch Eakins' career by being exhibited in a major show of art at the fair. He hoped that there, in view of thousands of people from all over the world, it would be praised as a masterpiece. The curators of the exhibit of American paintings thought otherwise. Several of Eakins' smaller pieces were on display, but he was in for a great disappointment. *The Gross Clinic* was denied a place in the exhibit of art. Instead, *The Gross Clinic* was hung in another building altogether, in the corner of the pristine replica of a Civil War army field hospital.

The Gross Clinic was "exiled to the wall of the first-aid station," as one observer has commented, not quite accurately.[5] But the comment does capture Eakins' sense that his painting was read as a medical story and not as a work of art. In fact, it has always been seen since as importantly both. At the time, what was to have been a triumph turned into a deeply disillusioning experience for an artist mistaken for an illustrator.

Since then, the painting has become perhaps the most studied of all Eakins' work. Eakins might be amused to find *The Gross Clinic* treated as almost a holy icon. The painting hangs today in a shrine, a virtual chapel behind a bronze gate at Dr. Gross's Jefferson Medical College. But as reverently as it is treated, *The Gross Clinic* is still a medical school's trophy. Only when it is on public exhibition, as it was in 1982 in Boston, can it be fully appreciated as a powerful work of art.

A May Morning in the Park (The Fairman Rogers Four-in-Hand), 1879–80.
(Philadelphia Museum of Art)

VIII

WORKSHOP

A GREAT CHAMPION OF American writers got the painter right. In *American Renaissance*, F. O. Matthiessen, likening Eakins to Thoreau and Whitman, notes that the painter "even shied away from words that seemed pretentious, preferring to say 'workshop' instead of 'studio,' 'painter' instead of 'artist,' 'naked' instead of 'nude'"[1] Thomas Eakins went into his workshop to teach students to paint in the spring of 1874. His friend Earl Shinn had the idea that Gérôme's best student would make a good teacher for his fellow members of the Sketch Club and got the ball rolling. This club had as its members gentlemen of Philadelphia, both amateur artists and would-be professional artists who came together to draw. Serious about the undertaking, the club had studios on one of the narrow streets below Broad Street and its members hoped to start a life drawing class. In a modest letter, Eakins accepted his nomination to teach. (There doesn't seem to have been any mention of money in the negotiations.)[2]

Eakins was not a member himself, but he plunged in and proved to be a true teacher from the start. Shinn, proud of his choice, reported that

Tom was "not only [a] . . . thorough master of his subject, but that he had a distinct genius for teaching of his subject." After a year, Eakins told his friend that his "boys," some of whom were older than he, "were getting on very well. . . . Some are very earnest. But some continue to make the very worst drawing ever was seen." After two years, the class seemed sufficiently established and successful that several enthusiastic members petitioned the Pennsylvania Academy of the Fine Arts to add life drawing to its curriculum in what was to be a reinvigorated art school.[3]

In 1876, the academy moved into an audaciously handsome new building, designed by Frank Furness, at Broad and Cherry streets. From the start, the museum was the home of some of the finest paintings of the new republic, the work of the Peales, Charles and his son Rembrandt; Benjamin West; and William Rush. With the nation celebrating its centennial in Philadelphia that year, it was a propitious time for unveiling what was clearly to be one of the city's major buildings. Though it now seems an aged dowager of architecture, the building remains impressive.

At the opening, proud Philadelphians could mount the grand central staircase to be in the company of the city's cherished paintings. An argument could be made that the country's first hundred years were better spoken for by these paintings than by the vast celebration of the nation's industrial might that dominated the exposition's halls, to the neglect of works of art.

The art students worked below this grandeur in sensible large studios ringed by plaster casts of classical statuary, lit by vast north-facing windows. Christian Schussele, the Alsatian artist who had conducted classes when Eakins was a student, was the dedicated and conservative chief instructor of the new school. He was joined by a professor of anatomy, William W. Keen of the Jefferson Medical School, who came equipped with a doctorate in medicine. Professional artists, several of whom conducted classes, and advanced amateurs comprised the "academicians and associate members" of the academy. Individuals with some artistic training could apply for admission tickets to the studios and classes; beginners were advised to get basic instruction before applying.

John Wright, at the Art Students' League of Philadelphia, c. 1889.
(The Pennsylvania Academy of the Fine Arts)

Life drawing was a touchy subject for the trustees of the academy. They inched toward admitting it to the sacred halls; no one under twenty-one was allowed to draw nude females. And there was a conflict over *who* should model. Should they be respectable men and women if they were to be in the company of art students from respectable

Philadelphia families? Or could men and women interested less in respectability than in a bit of cash be recruited? The board of directors worried whether members of the slightly bohemian Sketch Club should be invited to take life drawing, even though they had been its instigators. After all, the academy was a pillar of polite culture. When the classes began, Eakins and five of his students were the only ones from the Sketch Club class issued tickets to the studios, where scores of academy students worked.[4]

Once inside the academy, Eakins was quick to become both a student and an informal, unpaid instructor of his fellow artists. He went to work drawing like the others, but he often left his own easel to look at others' work, make suggestions, and prod student artists to see in a new way. Rather than have the artists at respectable distance from the models, Eakins urged them to prowl around to see the model from all angles and discuss with him the problems and possibilities posed by the human body.

This familiarity, seen by some as brazen, was the first principle of Eakins' theory of art instruction.[5] The directors of the academy, uneasy as they were about the bridging of a discreet distance between artist and model, had to admit that the work improved in quality. Meanwhile, Eakins, as Doctor Keen's assistant, led the laboratories in dissection with his usual gusto: his enthusiasm for the living body carried over to the dead. (Dissections were thought as essential to the training of the artist as it was to the education of the physician.) Cadavers, for which there was a flourishing market, were brought into the studios, along with the carcasses of animals. Students, with differing degrees of fervor, took saw and knife and tore apart, ligament by ligament, the detached arm or leg to find out how it had worked, while their fellows carved into head, chest, and belly of the torso in question.

The study of anatomy in the professor's studio was hardly a refined exercise. One ghoulish photograph shows a group of male students, knives in hand, eagerly at work dissecting a corpse's torso, while two colleagues hammer away on a detached arm. The women did not all shy away from this part of the anatomy course. Elizabeth Macdowell a long-

Women's modeling class at the Pennsylvania Academy of the Fine Arts,
c. 1882. (The Pennsylvania Academy of the Fine Arts)

time Eakins student and never a shrinking violet, put up a good feminist protest. "Dear Tom," she comfortably wrote, "I write to know if the
mornings of our days in the dissecting room can be secured to us exclusively. Up to the present the boys have worked on a new subject, while
we at ours; but now besides the fact that ours is dried up completely,
they have cut off the head, arms and scapulii [sic] so the back, about the
freshest part is about useless. This was done without consulting us and
Miss Robert and I had just prepared it for study."

Elizabeth Macdowell was not unique in her eagerness to be totally
involved in her education as a painter, and her informal manner with
her teacher is indicative of Eakins' teaching style and the drive of the
female students. Rather than simply waiting to get married, these
women were willing to breach barriers and abandon ladylike pursuits to
achieve that goal. It took a good deal of resolve for women to be admit-

ted in the academy, but they were. Eakins championed his female students, saw them as equals to the male students, and demanded from them just as much as he did from the men.

The core of any painter's training in Eakins' time (as is still true) was to know how to draw and, in the academy's case, the bulk of the work was to be done from plaster casts of classical sculpture. Repudiating much of his own earlier experience as a student, Eakins had long lost patience with this use of static stand-ins for the human form. After all, the casts of even "the best Greek period" were only imitations of human bodies. For Eakins, there was no substitute for the immediacy of a living body and the problem of translating a three-dimensional figure onto a two-dimensional piece of paper. Pointing to the plaster casts of classical art, he told his students that the statues were modeled from life. The human body was as beautiful in their day as it had been in the Athens of Phidias. This was Eakins' overarching manifesto.

Again departing from his own experience as a student, Eakins wanted his students to put down pencil and charcoal and work directly in color. To him, the outline of the figure was the least important thing; the students should get immediately to the wholeness of the subject. One later student, Alexander Stirling Calder (father of the twentieth-century sculptor) recalled his first day in the life class, after working from casts; "Everyone was painting and I recall distinctly my first criticism from Eakins; I had begun to draw in charcoal, and when he saw what I was doing, he advised me to start painting immediately, saying, 'Attack all your difficulties at once.' I acquired a crazy old kit of oils and began to paint 'ghosts,' colorless things.

"Eakins was then the idol of the school," Calder continued, "at least that part of it that I met, the men. During rests, the class lounged at the foot of the stairs . . . and he often talked with us informally about methods and showed us a few simple gymnastic feats."[6] In short, he was an unorthodox and brilliant teacher and a wonderfully crazy character who was able to be totally uninhibited with his students. Even as they were terrified and humiliated, they loved him.

Charles Bregler, a devoted student, took notes in class one day in

1887 that yield a stream of his teacher's aphorisms: "Strain your brain more than your eye: You draw by the things that are easiest: Draw by the longest lines you see, then you put in the little knobs and swellings: Look at the whole figure at one time: You don't try to get any thing right the first time, you guess at it, then correct it: You want to go at a thing as simple as possible." There was advice that Eakins himself took; he told his students, "Get down your highest light, then your shadow, then work in between them until you get them harmonious. Don't go at it by putting a little here and a little there." In one fragment, Bregler caught Eakins' marriage of two worlds: "All the sciences are done in a simple way, in mathematics the complicated things are reduced to simple things."[7]

Eakins had intense relationships with his charges, primarily with the men. The out-of-class country outings he took students on were exclusively male. Only a fine line (not infrequently crossed) separates a deep involvement between teacher and student and a sexual connection of the two. The wise teacher, supposedly the more mature of the two, knows enough to keep to the correct side of the line and avoid emotional damage. Even if the urge for sex is strong, as it may well have been in Eakins' case, it can be resisted.

Eakins' behavior in general was not what is ordinarily deemed appropriate to teacher-student relations. At times he was boorish, even gross, to the dismay of some students, the delight of others—those who got the signal. When a Masonic lodge held a gala in the academy gallery, a dead horse slated for dissection appeared on the grand staircase.

Eakins did not himself fully practice what he preached about letting oneself go in painting. He took pains to portray his subject in exactly the properly proportioned boat or with the bow exactly right on the cello, but the basic tenet was as sound for him as for his students: with the mastery of anatomy, a painter could ensure accuracy and allow for the sculler or the cellist to appear as free as nature itself. One student reflected sixty years later, after transferring to the academy having read an article about Eakins' teaching methods, "Eakins' method of teaching [had] broken away from the stilted type of Academic training, and the students painted without preliminary drawing, using the brush only. . . . All this appealed . . . to me because of its radical character and thoroughness."[8]

Eakins might not have been willing to admit it, but he loved to teach and the Academy of the Fine Arts provided the opportunity. The directors of the academy were penny-pinchers when it came to spending money on salaries for their instructors, and Eakins was in danger of letting himself be exploited. When the directors were about to cease paying the salary of Christian Schussele, now old and infirm, and ease him out, Eakins, loyal to his first teacher, agreed to teach without pay if Schussele could receive his regular salary and be allowed to come in and give critiques of students' work. (How the Eakins family budget could sustain this degree of altruism is a tribute to Benjamin Eakins' still mysterious financial sagacity and to his generosity.)

In 1878, the directors of the academy realized they had a teacher with an international reputation and named him assistant professor; a year later he was made professor, taking Schussele's place. Like any good teacher, Eakins was a subversive who made the administration nervous, but as long as Fairman Rogers was the director in charge of instruction, Eakins did not have to worry. Unlike almost every distinguished man that Eakins came to know in Philadelphia, Rogers was rich and socially upper class. Rogers was also a scholar, a professor at the university, and later a trustee, but scarcely a typical academic. A fan of the aristocratic sport of driving a coach and four, Rogers and his friends were the subject of the only canvas for which Eakins can be accused of a society painting.

A May Morning in the Park of 1879–80 is one of Eakins' most exuberant sports pictures, with Rogers at the reins of his four-in-hand, driving a splendidly dressed lady, under a red parasol—a touch of color that was characteristic of Eakins's work—and top-hatted gentlemen through Fairmount Park. Eakins' scientific bent is in evidence; the smaller front wheels of the coach are a blur while the larger back wheels are clearer as they rotate more slowly. Eakins' later analytical work on motion is foretold in the work on the horses, whose legs move with anatomical precision. Rogers was sophisticated; he understood and admired Eakins, as more timid directors of the academy did not. As long as Rogers was a director of the academy, Eakins' job was secure.

In the academy studio with his students, Eakins was a scruffy lion prowling the savannah ready to pounce on a terrified gazelle. As the students tried to figure their instructor out they caucused; "one young lady," one of them reported, "was doing her work just fine, or trying to. . . ." When Eakins "looked at her picture, [he] asked what she was trying to make. She pointed to the model. He said he could not see it. Looked all around the room to find it. Finally, she had to get up and touch [the model] so that he could see which [object she was drawing]."[9] Whether then or on her disconsolate way home she understood Eakins' brutal critique, the reporter, Horatio Shaw, doesn't say.

His students' quest to understand Eakins was constant. Shaw, writing home and new to the studio, had gotten an inkling. He was advised by another to "hang right to it and the first thing you know you will draw well and won't know how it came about." He said that "Eakins used to go for him rough shod. Once he came up, took his paper off the board and crumpled it up in his hand, then looking at it says it looks like a piece of crumpled paper, intimating, I suppose, that it was not a drawing but better look like a piece of crumpled paper than nothing."[10]

Three months after entering Eakins' studio, Shaw reported that he had sketched an outline to a body, was satisfied with it, and ready to start painting. Then Eakins came along: "All that outlining don't [sic] amount to any thing it takes so much time let me show you how to commence[,] took my pallet which by the way I had all fixed up to my satisfaction [and] smeared my tints into another making a terrible mess of it then puting [sic] a broad lick of the brush here and there paying no attention to my outline and with not much regard for color smeared over my fine background and let what he calls foundation to build up on as he did once before in charcoal."[11]

Another struggler wrote that Eakins had "short hair and black eyes and [was] very peculiar in his way. Says but little. He will sit down, shove your picture toward the model, half-close his eyes, study it for a minute and if you are inclined to do this nice, pretty sort of drawing, he is most sure to take a piece of charcoal and smear it all over. He will put a great daub here and another there and then rubs away with his fingers for the half-tints, paying no attention to your pretty correct outline." Here the teacher is explaining his own work. An Eakins portrait is correct, a perfect likeness, "but never solely that. The expression will always exceed correctness and what's more, will have the feel that," as he told a student, "it would look right in case you would go around to the sides and back of it." Eakins had succeeded in translating the three-dimensional model to the two-dimensional paper or canvas.

Lonely in a strange city, Horatio Shaw set out on the weekend for a long walk and, on Sunday, experienced Philadelphia at its most devout: he went to John Wanamaker's vast eccentric department store. The Depot, as it was titled, appeared to be an oriental railroad station that had counters and aisles radiating from its circular center. Being the lord's day, the store was closed, but the building stayed open to house the merchant prince's Sunday school. At the far end of the structure, the pipe organ that played for Wanamaker's customers, "overwhelmingly Protestant and white" during the week, now played hymns for the Sabbath scholars. Never had Horace Shaw experienced anything like it, and you wonder how he could reconcile the madcap of Thomas Eakins' studio with John Wanamaker's piety.[12]

Eakins clearly was a teacher who gave his all to his students and left a powerful mark on them, but a school of Eakins never developed. The question arises whether his influence opened the door of these students' creativity, or closed it. Does such a committed teacher draw forth from even unlikely students work they did not know they were capable of, or does he intimidate his students to the extent that they never achieve the work of which they might have been capable? These thoughts, of course, beg the question of what that capability consists. Eakins' successor, Thomas Anschutz, a less talented painter than he, had students who formed what is known as the Ash-Can School. The paintings of these talented artists owed little to the example of Anschutz's work. Paradoxically, Eakins' rigorous insistence that his method of painting was correct was at odds with his creed of personal freedom, and may have cramped the imaginations of his devoted students. Robert Henri, perhaps the best of the Ash-Can painters, was a great admirer not of his teacher, but of Eakins. Perhaps it was Eakins' paintings that did his best teaching.

The Cello Player, 1896. (The Pennsylvania Academy of the Fine Arts)
See color plate 8.

IX

PAINTER AND SCIENTIST

THOMAS EAKINS, THIRTY-SIX and fit, was in his prime in 1880. Notice had been taken. The previous spring he had been elected to the Society of American Artists. Smith, a new women's college in Massachusetts, had bought *In Grandmother's Time*, a sentimental piece, but Eakins had finally made his first sale. Never was he more self-confident as an artist. To become known in New York, he gave the Metropolitan Museum *The Chess Players*. Two bright and lively paintings, *A May Morning in the Park* and *The Biglin Brothers Turning the Stake-Boat*, had been accepted for the fall show at the academy. The opening reception every year was a major social event in Philadelphia. All of the city's grandees would attend, but none would look at Eakins' paintings—or any others—that night. On simpler days, other museum-goers would, making up, to a degree, for the fate of *The Gross Clinic* at the exposition.

Eakins' painting was going well and so was his teaching. His students adored him, or at least those whom he particularly liked did; and he had a steady job he liked. Thomas Eakins was ready to spread his wings. He

Eakins in his Chestnut Street studio, c. 1890.
(Philadelphia Museum of Art)

was, in fact, immensely busy in the 1880s. He taught regularly at the academy, for five academic years he commuted to Brooklyn to teach at that city's Art Guild, and he was painting.

One break from teaching was a commission that many artists would have coveted. In 1877, with another Civil War general moving into the White House, the Union League of Philadelphia commissioned Eakins to paint President Rutherford B. Hayes. Samuel Bell of the league wrote Hayes in June asking for his permission to sit for Eakins. Hayes was busy at the time sending troops to quell striking workers in Pittsburgh and had no time to sit. The president suggested that Eakins work from a

photograph, but the painter told Bell: "I do not intend to use any photographs." Suppression of the workers behind him, Hayes agreed to sit.
Eakins took the train to Washington in the stifling heat. At the White
House, waiting for the president, he sketched Lafayette Park until Hayes
would see him.[1]

In his letter to Bell, Eakins told us a great deal about how he worked.
He wanted to paint a full-figured portrait, but if pressed for time, would
settle for just the head, explaining that "a hand takes as long to paint as
a head nearly and a man's hand looks no more like another man's hand
than a head looks like another's" In either case, the price would be the
same, $400. When the two met, Hayes said brusquely that "a distin-
guished artist" needed only fifteen minutes for the sitting.[2] (William
Carl Browne's official portrait of the president looks it.)

They set up a studio in what is now called the Treaty Room and
Eakins went to work, but the task wasn't easy. "The President once
posed, I never saw him in the same pose again. He wrote, took notes,
stood up, swung his chair around," Eakins wrote to a friend. "In short, I
had to construct him as I would a little animal." To another friend, Will
Crowell's other sister, Kathrin, to whom he was thought to be roman-
tically inclined, he wrote, in the French that he still affected, "*Mon petit
[sic], Le president m'en donné deux sessions. Il a posé tres mal.*" (The president gave me two sessions. He posed very badly.) The finished work—
of Hayes' head only—was displayed in a Chestnut Street gallery in
Philadelphia and then at the Union League, where it disappeared.
When, late in life, Eakins went to see it, it couldn't be found. One rumor
was that the "rubicund countenance" was thought to be troubling to
Hayes' teetotaler wife, Lucy.[3]

Thomas Eakins, though he never used the words, had a democratic
American art in mind. His view of who populated that America was
narrow. It stretched only to include Fairman Rogers's coach and four on
one end of the spectrum and the black men who poled Eakins through
the marshes to shoot rail on the other. That was as far from an all-white
world as he ever strayed, and fishermen at work with their nets were the
only workmen of any color he would paint. On the other hand, there

were no celebrities whom he chose to paint. Eakins had painted men busy at athletics, a surgeon in the midst of an operation, one sister ready to go skating, one sister playing the piano and another, the baby, playing with her toys. Still ahead were singers performing, a cellist playing, a physics professor in his laboratory. All were inhabitants of a professional world, of people alert and active in a busy America.

Eakins also had a wonderful place to retreat from that busyness. His old schoolmate Will Crowell, now his brother-in-law, decided in 1872 to give up his city law practice. Will and Fanny moved to a 113-acre farm in Avondale, a town in the lovely country roughly forty miles southwest of Philadelphia. Will tended the cattle and the feed crops, while Fanny, in addition to producing ten children in the next twenty years, oversaw the infirmary as her brood came down with the dangerous ailments besetting children in the nineteenth century, tended the always busy kitchen, raised the vegetables for the household—and got up at four to practice at her piano.

If it was not unmitigated Eden for the Crowells, it was for Fanny's brother. Tom, taking advantage of the rail line that ran out from Philadelphia to a stop near the farm, spent large amounts of time in Avondale. It became an essential part of his life; his brother-in-law even provided him with a studio in the attic. (Fanny sometimes commandeered it to sequester a child with a contagious disease; James, the last surviving of the children, recalled when not feeling very well having to duck the dangling skeleton of Eakins' defunct pet monkey to reach this asylum.[4]

In the summer of 1880, Eakins bought himself a camera. Manufacturers were competing with models that were relatively portable. His was a Scovill, a wooden affair that took 4×5 glass plates and had detachable lenses.[5] A wooden box containing the lenses was lugged along with the tripod and the black hood that covered the photographer's head while he took the picture and moved the exposed plate to the light-secure box. Eakins was caught up in a craze that he had first known as a student in Paris where everyone, it seemed, was either taking photographs or looking at them. But, true to form, Eakins wasn't interested in simply being an amateur with a new gadget. He soon turned to the serious use of photography. Now, with his own camera, he set out to make pictures that would celebrate the world as he wanted it to be.

The Eakins family went to Manasquan on New Jersey's Atlantic coast the next summer and Tom took his first landscape photographs of the surf rolling onto the beach. Unlike his later work, these pictures do not feature people. Later that year, Eakins used his camera to assist in the preparation of pictures of shad fishermen pulling seines full of fish from the Delaware River; in one of these paintings, a group of very properly clad people watch them at their work. Eakins took several photographs of the fishermen. Choosing the best, he used it as the image for his painting. Though he found the fishermen satisfactory for his painting, he was dissatisfied with the onlookers. He took another photograph of some of his family and friends posed precisely in relationship to the scene as the earlier group had been. Eakins then painstakingly used the two photographs to transfer reference points, with minute lines and checks onto the canvas. Viewers of the completed painting, *Shad Fishing at Gloucester on the Delaware River*, would have had no reason to think that the scene was a composite of two images.[6]

In the late twentieth century, several Eakins paintings were the subject of painstaking analytic study using infrared readings. The readings exposed a sort of tracing, a line of pinpoints used to place Eakins' subjects. This method was distressing to some scholars, who saw it as cheating, but intriguing to others, who marveled at the artist's skillful use of photography. After all, the tracing hints were exactly that; assistance in the preparation of beautifully rendered oil paintings. Eakins' painterly imagination was expanded by his camera, but it was still a painter's imagination. In *Shad Fishing*, Eakins' favorite setter, Harry, is not where the photograph has him, but where the painter wants him, lying on the sandy shore of the calm river.[7]

There has been considerable interest in Eakins' use of this pinpoint technique. In a major retrospective opening in Philadelphia in 2001, a good deal of wall space was devoted to showing, through infrared enlargements, how Eakins worked. Many thought it pedantic and distracting; others found it fascinating. An entire chapter in the massive

Shad Fishing at Gloucester on the Delaware River, 1881.
(Philadelphia Museum of Art)

catalogue is devoted to this technique. A new understanding of Eakins'
technique was achieved, but better still, this exhaustive research
reopened the discussion of Vermeer's use of the camera obscura. Those
who thought Eakins was somehow cheating found that he was in the
best of company.

Shad fishing fascinated Eakins; the only paintings we have of workingmen are of fishermen hauling their seines in the Delaware River, or
mending their nets on a low hilltop. These men took their living from
waters that fed Eakins' imagination, whether the calm Schuylkill surface
on which oarsman raced or the Delaware with its bountiful marshes or
its waters on which he sailed. In his early family pictures done at home
and the sporting pictures set in the wonderful outdoors, Eakins gives no
hint that he is anything other than the most respectable of painters. The
naked body is never on display. Whether his family and friends posed
indoors or out, they were clad, even hatted, as is the man at the tiller in
the sailboat.

Thomas Eakins had a wonderful way of tangling up his many enthusiasms. His ally on the academy board of directors, Fairman Rogers, heard of Eadweard Muybridge's photographic motion studies in California, and informed Eakins. When Muybridge was in town being recruited by Rogers, a trustee of the University of Pennsylvania, and the provost, William D. Pepper—the senior officer of Benjamin Franklin's school did not use the title of president—Eakins wasted no time inviting the scientist who studied how bodies moved to give two lectures to his anatomy course at the academy.

Pepper, a prescient scholar and a university head willing to spend money, had picked up the pieces of a battle between the prickly Muybridge and Leland Stanford, his patron, and lured the promising scientist to Philadelphia. Muybridge was an exceedingly ambitious scientist, who, like scores of others, sought to expand the world of photography to include motion.*

Muybridge was given the funds (ultimately, $40,000—an enormous grant at the time) and space on the campus to complete an expanded study of the locomotion of animals, humans included. In the yard of the veterinary school he saw to the construction of a shed 120 feet long, the back wall of which was painted black. Its front "wall" was a series of vertical and horizontal white strings, somehow made taut, which formed two-inch squares. Some feet away was a facing shed 32 feet long in which twenty-four cameras were set up on tripods or firm bases. A portable camera was available to assist in the experiment of capturing on film the almost continuous motion of the gait of horses of the Gentlemen's Driving Club. Animals were recruited from the Philadelphia Zoo, and human models (including a willing Thomas

---

*Who was first? Eadweard Muybridge is credited with being the father of the motion picture, but hundreds of people fascinated with what might be done to get motion into photography had made critical experiments in the nineteenth century, including Thomas Eakins. In that great age of tinkering, dozens of persons contributed ingenious equipment that, bit by bit, resulted in the perfection of a practical cinema.

Eakins) came from the academy, track and field athletes from the university, and even deformed patients from the university hospital.

Pepper, himself a physician, in 1884 headed a committee "to insure [the experiment's] thoroughly scientific character," consisting of professors of anatomy, physics, veterinary anatomy and pathology, dynamical engineering (William D. Marks, another friend of Eakins), civil engineering, and physiology. As a mark of his standing, Eakins was named to the committee, the only nonscientist on it other than Edward Horner Coates, the academy's new chairman of the instruction committee, who had his eye not only on science, but on his unpredictable art teacher.

Eakins' participation in the experiment was not confined to being an interested onlooker or a model willing to take off his clothes and run the gauntlet in front of the camera engineer. No amateur getting in the way around the edges of Muybridge's work, Eakins conducted experiments that rivaled the Englishman's famous work. Aware of the work of many experimenters in Europe, Eakins utilized and modified the wheel camera of Etienne Jules Marcey, "perfecting it greatly" in the view of Marks, who later wrote part of the formal report on Muybridge's study. Eakins designed and, presumably with Marks's engineering help, built a wheel camera that used not a single plate, but spun two plates, which enhanced the recording of the action on which it was focused.

When the work was complete, the provost published the findings; the fascinating result was *Animal Locomotion: The Muybridge Work . . . The Method and the Result*. In one of the essays, Harrison Allen, a physiologist, credited Eakins' work, treating him throughout as a fellow scientist. In another essay, Professor Marks writes generously of the participants, including Muybridge's assistant, who might well have been overlooked. His references to Eakins are somewhat ambiguous, noting, "It is to be regretted that Professor Eakins's admirable work is not yet sufficiently completed for publication as a whole."[8]

Why don't we have a formal report of Eakins' contribution? For one thing, the science itself was fun—figuring out how to do it and then doing it—but writing up his findings, as scientists must, may never have

Thomas Eakins, *Motion Study: George Reynolds Nude, Pole-vaulting to Left*, c. 1885. (The Pennsylvania Academy of the Fine Arts)

appealed to him. He wasn't a word person and the way scientists used them was alien to his sensibilities. There may be another explanation; after all Marks could have helped with the writing. Self-centered, perhaps, Eakins was being touchy and did not want his experiments to be lumped in as a footnote in the publication of Muybridge's work, the nineteen magisterial folio volumes of pictures that constitute a landmark in photographic and cinematographic literature.

A third, more likely explanation is that, in the end, the artist was a scientist only to satisfy his own huge curiosity, and not to produce a scientific publication. He wanted to know what he, the other human models, and all those animals looked like in all their minute movements. He looked at those photographs the same way he looked at a cadaver or a model in various positions, and he wanted his students to do so as well. It was that endlessly fascinating human body that compelled Eakins' attention;

Mrs. Mary Arthur, 1900. (Metropolitan Museum of Art, New York)

the camera and the university research he had done were not to enhance science so much as to allow him to see even more acutely.

There is a precision to his handling of the human form in his paintings that is seldom equaled. Whether the baseball player at bat or, much later, the men standing for full-length portraits, the feet are always firmly planted under the subject. In 1900, Eakins painted *Mrs. Mary Arthur*, an elderly lady knitting. A century later, an alert physician noted that the hands holding the red yarn were arthritic. Astonished by the painter's accuracy, he made his diagnosis: "Mrs Arthur's left thumb is deformed. The base of the metacarpal is subdued dorsally and radically." Eakins would have been pleased, but not surprised by the finding. There is also the story of a teaching session when he and Tom Eagan, a student, were discussing Rembrandt's famous picture of black-clad Dutch doctors standing around the naked torso of a corpse. Eagan, brash as only students can be, said he didn't like the picture. Eakins agrees, but not on any aesthetic grounds. The body, said Eakins, the perfectionist, isn't lying correctly on the table, a critique of the painting that would not occur to many people.[9]

Writing in *The New Yorker* in 1982, Philip Hamburger said Eakins was "a stranger everywhere all his life." How can this square with the gregarious man engaged with leading scientists at the university? One of these, Professor William D. Marks, was a member of "Tom's Sunday Club." Eakins sought out Stewart Culin, a professor in the new field of anthropology who, in turn, introduced him to Frank Hamilton Cushing, the scholar of the Zuni, whom Eakins painted in full Zuni regalia, complete with his decidedly non-Zuni body, face, and hair. This man of so many interests was certainly no stranger to some of the most prominent intellectuals in Philadelphia.[10]

Just what was it that Hamburger had in mind? Was it that Eakins was a stranger in the physiological sense? As comfortable as Tom was with these men, there was still a barrier. He could go only so far in intimacy with men he assumed were strangers to his own sexual nature. In 1884, Tom found someone for whom he was not a stranger, with whom he could share, perhaps only silently, that which kept him at arm's length from others; he married Susan Macdowell.

The Artist's Wife and His Setter Dog, 1884–89.
(Metropolitan Museum of Art, New York)
See color plate 9.

X

SUE

SUSAN MACDOWELL EAKINS is an intriguing woman who has not been understood. If she is taken note of at all, it is as a loyal wife. One impression of her, after Tom's death in 1916, is that of a professional widow dedicated solely to keeping the frail fame of her husband alive, only to triumph when she made him famous with a donation of fifty of his pictures to the Philadelphia Museum of Art. In a still bleaker picture of her life, she is merely a wife in a barren marriage—there were no children—the victim of having married a homosexual. Susan Eakins was far more than either of these ungenerous descriptions would suggest.

Susan, born in 1851, was a Philadelphia girl, the daughter of William H. Macdowell, a man who had imagination and ambition for his daughters. As young women, Susan and her sister Elizabeth were both accepted into the academy studio program; Susan became one of Eakins' prize students. As she and Eakins worked together in his studio, they came to know each other well.

Tom Eakins is said to have been engaged to Kathrin Crowell in 1874, when he was thirty. The two were still not married when she died in 1879, which suggests a tragically lost love, or perhaps, a lack of ardor on the part of the would-be suitor, the would-be bride, or both.[1]

Tom wrote many affectionate letters to Kathrin Crowell, in answer to hers, when she summered on the Jersey shore each year. His reports on sports and his artistic progress read more like friendly notes rather than love letters. "I miss you very much" is as passionate as he gets. The engagement, if it existed, had been a product of what their respective families, already linked by marriage, expected of the two available young people.[2] Four years after Kathrin's death, Eakins had another bride in mind, one of his most talented students.

William Macdowell was a substantial citizen and unorthodox free-thinker whose striking face and wild hair caused his son-in-law to paint him several times. He, like John Sartain, was an engraver. As mentioned earlier, the craft was of great importance in the art world, when engraving was the only means of making copies of paintings available when the original was not at hand. Susan's mother, Hannah Gardner Macdowell, presided over a house whose table was set with fine silver and in whose parlor there was a piano. At the time of her marriage, Susan had five surviving siblings, three of whom were to live well into her old age.[3]

It was a marriage made not in heaven, but in Philadelphia by two adults fully understanding of each other. They were married on January 19, 1884. Susan was not yet thirty-three years old; Thomas would turn forty in six months. Although neither bride nor groom was a Friend, let alone associated with any church, they married "in the Quaker form."[4] Family and probably a few friends gathered in the Macdowells' Race Street house to witness Susan and Thomas vow to be man and wife. And a remarkable union it was. Tom's fascination with and affection for Sue is recorded in the many paintings and drawings of her, as well as countless photographs. The biographer's usual evidence of the nature of a marriage—diaries betraying yearning, letters declaring ardor—is missing in the case of the two Eakinses.[5] There is in fact a dismaying lack of record of Susan's life—dismaying because she is a fascinating woman vastly underrated as an artist.

Tucked away in the hodgepodge of material scooped up and saved from 1729 Mt. Vernon Street by the Eakins student and admirer Charles Bregler is an enigmatic entry folded into a wallet, copies of two passages from Whitman's *Leaves of Grass*. It appears to be written by Sue, though her hand is remarkable similar to Tom's. Regardless of which one of this remarkable couple chose these passages to quote verbatim, they speak to the ambiguity of Sue and Tom's relationship.

> Her shape arises,
> She less guarded than ever,
> The gross and soiled, she moves among does not make her
>   gross and soiled,
> She knows the thoughts and as she passes, nothing is con-
>   cealed from her,
> She is none the less considerate or friendly therefore,
> She is the best beloved, it is with out exception, she has no
>   reason to fear and she does not fear,
> Oaths[,] quarrels, hiccupped songs, smutty or [illegible word]
>   are idle to her as she passes,
> She is silent, she is possessed of herself, they do not offend her,
> She receives them as the laws of Nature[,] she is strong,
> She too is a law of Nature, there is no law stronger than she is.[6]

Then on the next page, as if written on another occasion, with a different pen, the writer continues,

> my dear friend, my love was coming O then I was happy I heard the waters roll slowly up the shore, I heard the hissing rustle of the liquid and sands as directed to me whispering to congratulate me, for the one I love most lay sleeping by me under the same cover on the cool night. In the stillness as the autumn moonbeams his face was inclined toward me and his arm lies lightly around my breast—and that night I was happy.[7]

What are we to make of all this? The Whitman passages suggest a silent conversation that Sue and Tom had for the length of their long marriage. Each of them could know of the other's love for someone of their own sex and love each other the more for knowing.

Susan was not simply the keeper of the flame, but a discerning critic who knew the value of the work her husband had left and was determined to achieve public recognition of how great a painter Thomas Eakins was. But that fact hardly does credit to either the woman or the wife that she was. Today we would fault her for abandoning her own career in order to foster his. We would want her in the studio at the other easel doing the fine paintings that she was capable of. Those works, few in number, were largely done after his death.[8]

The Eakinses made a remarkable success of a thirty-two-year marriage that was in many ways unorthodox. Neither Sue nor Tom appear to have been particularly attracted sexually to the other, yet they managed this troubling fact with great grace. What enabled them to do so? They were truly great friends. (What precisely the nature of their sexual history with each other was, no one can be sure.) They respected each other's artistic ability, although there was a little condescension on his part and a corresponding lack of confidence on hers. He was interested in photography; so was she. He could look at one of his half-finished paintings and judge it; she could do so even better. If his canvas was vast, as in *The Agnew Clinic*, she assisted in painting the onlookers, slipping Tom in among the students.

They were both fond of animals. A late photograph, one of the few taken of them together, shows Sue playing with their dog. They went together to the theater and the opera; one year they attended opening night at the Chestnut Street Opera House. At other performances they heard *Aida* and *Rigoletto* and, at the theater, they saw Edwin Booth and Helena Modjeska playing in *Hamlet*, *The Merchant of Venice*, Sarah Bernhardt playing in *La Dame aux Camélias*, and Richard Mansfield in *Peer Gynt*.

When Tom was away from Philadelphia, his letters reveal that he missed his wife greatly, and allow us to see what being married to

Thomas Eakins was all about. When, for example, he was working in Maine, it was she who saw to it that his bicycle, which he was loath to be without, was sent to him; when he went off on one of his strange sessions photographing his students nude, she took over the camera so that he could be in the picture. Most of all, Susan aided and abetted her husband as he filled 1729 Mt. Vernon Street with an ever expanding menagerie. Snakes, a monkey—not her favorite (it bit)—caged birds, fish, and, most important of all, Harry the red setter, had to stand in for absent children.

I am wrong to say there is little evidence of the nature of their relationship: it is to be found in their paintings and sketches of each other. In 1884 and 1885 Eakins produced what can only be described as a lovely painting of his wife sitting demurely in a blue dress, looking thin, even fragile—which she was not. What he achieved in the portrait is the effect of an affectionate exchange between the sitter and the artist.

Tom painted many portraits of Susan, the greatest of which is on the wall of the Hirshhorn Museum in Washington. In this work, the full depth of the woman is before us. There is not a stroke of glamour in the painting; there is only the great beauty caught by someone who not only loves but understands her. And she him. In moments of great strain, Sue gave ballast to a pitching ship.

Nothing tells us more about Susan and Tom's relationship than a simple drawing by Susan on a blackboard that, miraculously, someone photographed. In it, Eakins and his closest friend, Sam Murray, are setting off on their ever-at-hand bicycles for one of their frequent, determined rides. Their rumps grip bicycle seats, their backs—Tom's the rounder— arch forward; they are already pedaling madly. Susan has caught Tom and Sam in humorous, loving detail.

In the Philadelphia Museum of Art there is a room devoted entirely to Eakins' work. Hung prominently on a panel in the passageway into this room is Susan's portrait of her husband. Her rendering of his body, stuffed in a suit as he is in his painting, may not be quite as true as the one Tom achieved, but there is a greatness to hers that more than

Blackboard drawing by Susan Macdowell Eakins of Thomas Eakins and
Samuel Murray on bicycles. (Courtesy of Harvard University Fine Arts
Library, from Margaret McHenry, *Thomas Eakins Who Painted*)

matches his. It is, to be sure, derivative; she has studied at the master's hand and this, of all her work, is the painting that speaks most of Eakins' influence. She has mastered the master and given us the immense sadness of the man she loves.

But this is to get us ahead of our story. Much was to transpire before that sadness was to play so large a part in these lives.

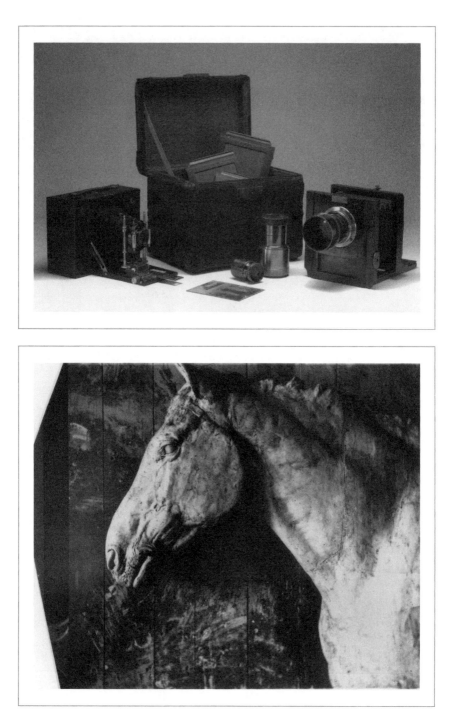

Eakins' Scovill camera and equipment.
(Hirshhorn Museum and Sculpture Garden)
Plaster Model of Clinker for an Equestrian Relief of General Grant, 1892.
(Bryn Mawr College, Canaday Library, Seymour Adelman Collection)

XI

SCULPTURE AND PHOTOGRAPHY

THOMAS EAKINS HAD been intrigued by anatomy when he was still a teenager. He began to study the subject seriously at the Jefferson Medical College at the same time that he was getting his first studio experience at the Academy of the Fine Arts. He was still at it in 1880 when he made somewhat ghoulish bronze castings of actual dissected human parts—a right arm and shoulder; a left thigh, leg, and foot; and the back torso of a dissected male.

Eakins made similar castings of horse carcasses and became one of the finest of equine sculptors. Years later, at the Avondale farm, using his own horse, Billy, as a model, he built the complex full-size frame on which he molded and then had cast in bronze the horse on which Abraham Lincoln rides side by side with Ulysses S. Grant at the 1895 Soldiers' and Sailors' Memorial Arch in Brooklyn. That splendid monument to the victorious north in the Civil War makes no bones about who won that war; Eakins sculpted no Traveler for an appropriately absent Robert E. Lee. After a considerable hunt for a horse to stand in for Grant's equally famous Cincinnati, a neighbor of the Crowells, A. J. Cassatt (father of

Mary), lent his Clinker for the task. (Grant, the business failure once more in debt to a generous industrial magnate, thus rides the horse of a president of the Pennsylvania Railroad.) Eakins' friend William R. O'Donovan, ironically a Confederate veteran from Virginia, made the sculptures of Grant and Lincoln (which are inferior to those of the horses they ride).[1]

In 1880, Eakins made his first oil painting of a nude figure, *The Crucifixion*. The subject itself is an unlikely one for a nineteenth-century freethinker. Eakins had seen Zubarán's similar study at the Prado, but, in terms of influence on Eakins' work, we must think of the portraits of Velázquez. The art student had seen innumerable Renaissance pictures of crucifixions. Growing up in a Protestant segment of Philadelphia, Eakins as an art student saw a vast array of sixteenth- and seventeenth-century Catholic religious paintings in Madrid and Seville. He was impressed, but not it would seem, eager to emulate these. His second Paris teacher, Léon Bonnat, who led him to portraiture, painted another crucifixion that Eakins knew. Now, ten years later, Eakins turned to that most standard subject; it was as if he said to himself that if so many artists had painted crucifixions, so should he.

This work is very unlike paintings of men mending nets or playing the cello. Crucifixions no longer carried the religious force in bourgeois nineteenth-century Philadelphia as they had in Zurbarán's day. (Only in the religion-ridden twenty-first has the tortured Christ made his controversial cinematic comeback in America.) If we had any evidence that Eakins had the smallest social consciousness, some enterprising mind might see the mutilated and dead body on a cross as an allegory of the work of the Ku Klux Klan, but the chalky figure certainly does not evoke a black man lynched and Eakins was not given to allegory.

Whatever possessed Eakins to do the painting, possessed he was. He set out in his usual thorough way to ensure realism. And here his dedication to the way things worked reached new heights. He hoisted some timbers onto the ferry, and, crossing the Delaware, led one of his favorite students, Laurie Wallace, into the wilds of New Jersey. They planted the cross, Wallace stripped, and, as he laconically reported the story fifty

Crucifixion, 1880.
(Philadelphia Museum
of Art)

years later, he was "beginning to pose when some hunters came along, so [we] went to a still more secluded spot." Eakins set the cross up, digging a hole in the ground for it, and Wallace got up on it. Remarking that "Eakins was thorough," Wallace recalled that he "had a crown of thorns" to wear as well. Eakins then "simply photographed" Wallace; "that was all."[2]

Precision of anatomy was what he was after. Fortunately, his thoroughness did not reach to nails and hammer and Wallace was given a little shelf on which to put his unbloodied feet. All of this bizarre business would seem unnecessary, but Eakins had to know how a body outstretched on a cross would look. The painting was done back in his studio. Eakins, in his usual conscientious way, portrays a corpse of convincing pallor. The resulting work is the hardest of Eakins' paintings to account for. If Eakins was reaching for a way to celebrate a particular naked body, Wallace, skinny and a bit slack, was an odd choice. Instead, Eakins, using Wallace's pose on the cross only to ensure anatomical accuracy, gave us a taut, imagined figure. Eakins has painted with his usual skill, but the result is a picture of a dead American boy disguised in the posture of a Renaissance Christ.[3]

Eakins married his fascination with anatomy to his infatuation with photography. After putting his camera to remarkable experimental use in working out plans for his paintings and to execute the motion studies, he turned to the more conventional business of taking people's pictures. Nude photography has been standard fare since the invention of the camera, but, discounting pornographers, Eakins must have set a record. There are some 400 nude photographs taken in the 1880s by Thomas Eakins and his students.

As an artist, Eakins wanted his students not merely to observe photographs of their fellows and of themselves naked. He wanted them to not only render their work with anatomical correctness, but also be comfortable with their bodies as they drew in the studio. Scores of pictures were taken; a good many ended up tacked on the wall of the studio as reference points. It saved students money—models weren't needed—but, more important, it taught a strangely expressed humanistic lesson, to be comfortable with freedom.

Eakins was more than willing to practice what he preached. There are a generous number of pictures of Professor Eakins nude. Candor, verging at times on exhibitionism, and not a little vanity, were on display. Well into his forties, Eakins had a body to be proud of. His full smooth torso, with sloped broad shoulders, stood atop not long but well-defined legs. Surely the most famous of these has him facing the camera cradling a full-bodied naked woman, her rounded hip held high enough to expose his generous penis. It is a graceful picture and, if categories are needed, a heterosexual one.

Another series of Eakins' photographs comprises charming pictures of his prepubescent nieces and nephews taken outdoors at Avondale. If these pictures were taken today they would probably be attacked by some as prurient. With our twenty-first-century hyperawareness of child abuse, much of it justified, eyebrows would rise. But this was not the twenty-first century, it was the nineteenth, well before Freud and, in so

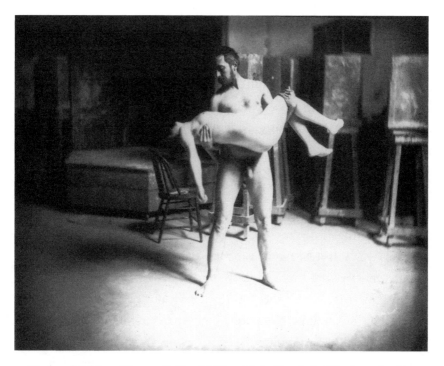

Circle of Eakins, *Thomas Eakins Holding Nude Female in His Arms, Looking Down*, c. 1883–85. (The Pennsylvania Academy of the Fine Arts)

many ways, less encumbered by sexual restraint. There is no evidence that those children's parents, Fanny and Will Crowell, reacted in any way other than being charmed by these pictures of their children. The children, troubled only by the interruption in their serious work—play— were otherwise comfortable being photographed by their favorite uncle.[4]

Two other groups of pictures are of a different character. The first were photographs taken in the studio; the second were taken outdoors. Not all of those shot in the studio fall in the category of teaching "instructive." There are many pictures of Eakins' naked students wrestling taken in the studio and still more of them out in a seemingly secluded glade, which if come upon, would have startled a passerby. One group of pictures is of young men posed with arms overhead, requiring the viewer to focus on their genitalia. Still another group of images shows naked, young students in contrived athletic poses, boxing, pretending to throw javelins, and a boy playing the flute in a Pan pose. Tom Eagan, for one, is an Adonis. The photographs taken outdoors have an almost comic quality; the photographer—Eakins—catches the antic quality of the activities. Surely the most suggestive (and humorous) nude photograph is of a tug-of-war. In the picture, the men are not touching one another, but as the energetic tugging on the rope progressed, each would inevitably be pressing his penis against the buttocks of the person in front.[5]

What are we to make of all of this? Many of the outdoors pictures have a sophomoric quality, suggesting a bucolic fraternity initiation fantasy. This was a time of the heroic male figure, but these skinny boys do not pass muster with those appearing in framed photographs in college gymnasiums. And, for all the posing, there is not much that is sexually arousing in the pictures. Not surprisingly, there are no women students in these outdoor gatherings. (There *are* photographs of Susan Eakins, seemingly taken in a secluded spot; in the best known of these her back faces the viewer as she leans on a horse.) What was on Eakins' agenda? An art critic who has studied these photographs sees Eakins trying to create a bohemian community with his students, one that will deliberately flout conventions of decency. But no attempt to read philosophy into these bizarre pictures is convincing.

Still other photographs, taken by a student (possibly Susan Macdowell, if more probably a male student) are of fellow students, Eakins, and his setter Harry swimming in a mill pond—or posing on the ruined rock dam projecting into the pond. One of these photographs, taken frontally, is a close approximation of what was to become Eakins' famous *Swimming*.

Swimming, 1884–85. (Amon Carter Museum)
See color plate 10.

XII

SWIMMING

"AKINS IS PAINTING a picture for Mr. Coates of a party of boys swimming." So reported Thomas Anschutz to Laurie Wallace, who was now pursuing a career in Chicago. Eakins was at work on what is perhaps his most important philosophical painting— and the least understood. As Stephen Greenblatt writes of Shakespeare's sonnets, "One of the startling effects of the best of these poems—a prime reason they have drawn madly fluttering biographical speculations like moths to a flame—is an almost painful intimacy." *Swimming* was Eakins' one such poem.[1]

Recently *Swimming* has been understood almost exclusively as autobiographical, evidence of Eakins' homosexuality. The artist is indeed in his own picture and there is "painful intimacy." Looking at the canvas we assume he is naked, but Tom is swimming a lazy breaststroke and we see only his head and shoulders as he gazes at his frankly naked students.[2]

Few people have taken the trouble to know the names of the other people in the picture; instead, they are seen as generalized objects of erotic desire and Eakins, gazing at them, partakes of this desire. He

almost certainly was, but that is far from all that can be seen in the painting. In our own time, it has been seemingly impossible to publish a book
celebrating homosexuality and not reproduce this picture. Worse still are
fleshy details excerpted from it, as evidence that Eakins was gay.

Tom Eakins had told a surgeon's story, some rowers', sailors', and fishermen's stories; now he had the confidence to tell a liberating story for
all of America. With his paintbrush, he would do what Whitman had
done in poetry with his *Song of Myself*. In 1884 Eakins had every confidence in his ability to make the world hear him, though the voice was a
quiet one. It is not a big picture, only three feet wide and two feet high.
Now safely contained in a wide gilt frame, it was Eakins' silent cry for a
more perfect world. *The Swimming Hole*, its original, distractingly folksy
name, is a lovely rural landscape. Beyond the pond's calm inviting water,
the sun hits the bucolic shore. Only Eakins and his students have sneaked
into Eden. One perceptive critic has noted the picture's "stillness."[3]

Unlike the shad fishing pictures, there are no observers, nor anyone
working here. The only sign of human intrusion is the stone wall on
which the young men sprawl and stand. A mill once stood here; now it
too has been banished. Six men, five students who know one another
well and their teacher, have found a secluded place to swim on a summer day. The warm sun feels good, the water cool; they are having fun.
The countryside is remote; the crumbling stone foundation of the long
gone mill is a convenient (if not very soft) place to catch the sun, jump
into the water. George Rutledge is diving in to join Eakins, the first one
in and an expert swimmer.[4]

There is an echo of Henry Thoreau here. Thomas Eakins, by painting the picture of his experience, comes close to the picture Thoreau
painted in words early in *Walden*: "I got up early and bathed in the
pond; that was a religious exercise, and one of the best things that I did."
Commenting on that passage, the philosopher Philip Cafaro states, "The
sacrament's power come from its bodily immediacy—what could be
more immediate than a plunge, first thing in the morning, into a clear,
cold pond?—and its ability to thrust us into a state of excitement and
awareness that it celebrates."[5]

Eakins would not have used the terms "religious" and "sacrament," to describe lazing in the water watching his students, though the words are close to apt for him as well. His plunge was not that early in the morning, nor would the water be that cold on a summer day with the sun well up. And yet, Tom had reached the same level of "bodily immediacy," and his "state of excitement and awareness" only heightened the fact that unlike Thoreau he was not alone, but introducing the students to the same awakening that swimming gave him. It is not the undoubted homoerotic component of the painting that is Eakins' message; it is instead the appeal for freedom, for something truly natural.

When Thoreau told his story in 1854, there were not many listeners. *Walden* sold few copies in his lifetime; millions worldwide have heard it since, and grasped his message. Few understood Eakins' story at the time he painted it; unlike Thoreau, many still don't hear it clearly. For Melville, the dream of what might have been was found on the far-off island of Typee; for Eakins at a swimming hole near home. For Melville, the death of his dream was being bound to a clerk's desk in New York, with *Billy Budd, Foretopman* hidden in a bottom drawer.

Eakins' picture had its own strange history. It was promptly and prominently shown in the academy's fall exhibit of 1885, identified as being owned by a director of the academy, Edward Coates. A good many people who saw it there did not understand it. Leslie Miller, a good friend of Tom, commented on the show's awards event, "Mr. Eakins has done some very strange things. . . . In nothing that he has done has his work been so persistently and inexcusably bad as in the landscapes which he has introduced as backgrounds for his figures," and he cites *Swimming* as an example. The next year it was shown at expositions, not primarily focused on art, in Louisville and Chicago and "garnered a resounding critical silence."[6]

The picture was apparently never again exhibited in Eakins' lifetime, nor was it treated well at 1729 Mt. Vernon Street; it wasn't on the wall in the parlor or shown to visitors to Eakins' studio. It would seem to be a picture that he would have taken to Camden to show to Walt Whitman when they met, but there is no mention of it. It seems to have been stacked against the wall. For Eakins, his song had gone sour.

Only after Eakins' death was there an exhibit of much of his work at the Metropolitan Museum of Art. *Swimming* was one of three works given pride of place. The curator had chosen well; it's a splendid example of Eakins' finest and most profound work. But it was not until 1941 that F. O. Matthiessen connected Eakins' painting to Whitman's line "Twenty-eight bathers bathe by the shore," without pursuing the similarity.[7] In both instances the bathers are not alone; there is "the handsome and richly dressed" woman watching from behind the blinds in Whitman. Eakins is not only watching from the corner of the painting, but has preceded the bathers into the water. By putting himself into the picture he richly enhances the intimacy of the scene. (Eakins is not in any of the preparatory photographs, which he probably took.)

Some gay critics have read the picture as a document that proves that the artist was "one of us," even to the point of triumphantly insisting on a sight line from Eakins to the diver's penis. No one any longer denies that the sensuous call of the picture is male to male. That does not make it any less a general humane expression of the "excitement and awareness" that Thoreau's experience provoked when he went for his swim. In part, Eakins' timing was off. It was only 150 years after Thoreau that the clearly sensuous nature of the painting was seen and discussed in terms that Eakins might have hoped.[8]

In his own time, he was not heard, but his message was of a particularly American freedom, one that included the sexual. In the 1850s, Emerson, Thoreau, and Whitman had, in their differing ways, tried to take Americans forward to a freedom for which nature was the metaphor. The path ahead was brutally blocked by the Civil War. At the dedication of the cemetery at Gettysburg, in which lay thousands of those who died in that war, Abraham Lincoln, eschewing nature, or rather extending it into politics, broadened the clause "All men are created equal," to embrace the former slaves whom that war was setting free. This was at the point when white America's commitment to a spiritual freedom was being diminished by the brutality of war. A hardened white citizenry, embracing instead a materialistic ethos, was soon to make a shambles of Lincoln's promise to African Americans.[9]

Eakins missed all of this. He went blithely on trying to achieve the prewar message of the writers of the 1850s, even as he knew little of their work. Whitman he admired, but there is no evidence that he had read Thoreau or Melville. It is likely that he at least had read Emerson.

Emerson called for a unique American literature for the new young republic. Thoreau found his place outside the conventional world, at Walden Pond, and Melville had to search at sea. Whitman was the last of these writers and his poetic call was the one closest to that of the painter. And this painter, like the composer Charles Ives, was not letting the quest fall only to the wordsmiths. Though not using the rhetoric of political theory, all of these nineteenth-century radicals took the Declaration of Independence seriously and they took as given the concept of equality. Like the founders, they had a narrow definition not only of man, but of his race. Of the Declaration's champions, the only writer who saw it to be inclusive of women and black Americans was Frederick Douglass. I would simply argue that Eakins, like these writers, dreamed of a world where the pursuit of happiness could be sought on his own terms. He had the naïve view that such happiness would inevitably be his; it was not to be. But his message is still there to be seen and several art critics have done so.

Arthur Danto looks at the painting and finds the proposition of equality given literal expression in *Swimming*, "the absence of clothing is a metaphor for the proposition that all men are created equal." Linda Nochlin sees in the work a "heady sense of escape from social constraint. . . . In the Eakins painting, democratic freedom is signified by the youthful male American body in the American landscape: to be American is at once natural and to have a privileged relation to Nature." For Aristotle, "each age has its own beauty" Peter Schjehahl reminds us. "In youth, it lies in possession of a body capable of enduring all kinds of contests . . . while the young man is himself a pleasant delight to behold."[10] Eakins' students were too lazy to win the full praise of the ancient Greek philosopher, but these contemporary critics—and many more of us—read *Swimming* as a call for freedom and beauty.

As gently and as subtly as was Shakespeare writing sonnets to be sung for his beloved, Eakins painted a love song. None of the men at the millpond would seem to be direct objects of his affection. Eakins' sonnet carries an erotic message, but not one that is an open book. Finally, in the deepest sense, only he can fully experience that swim. On the other hand, *Swimming* carries a universal message, even as we allow for his omission of women and indeed any people looking not like him. Eakins' love of men is not that of some fantasy orgy, but rather the reaching for, the achievement of, something devoid of restraint. The pond is free of any artifice, the painter is at one with a comforting nature, he has said yes to a world free of corruption. Just as such innocence has been violated in latter-day misreading, so too did the picture in Eakins' day become part of his own undoing.

Eakins was not given to expressions of political philosophy, but implicit in his love of freedom was a disavowal of power. Trying to say we can do better with our republic than turn it into an all-powerful empire does not seem to me a mistake. The oddities of some of those who stepped outside conventional binds make more sense than the realities we seem destined to live with. Emily Dickinson was certainly one of the strangest of the bunch:

> I took my Power in my Hand—
> And went against the World—
> 'Twas not so much as David—had—
> But I—was twice as bold—
> I aimed my Pebble—but Myself
> Was all the one that fell—
> Was it Goliath—was too large—
> Or was myself—too small?[11]

Thomas Eakins' paintbrush was his sling. His Goliath was to be the Academy of the Fine Arts, indeed the whole of Philadelphia—of

America. Rather than setting society free, Eakins folded his own tent, and was never to paint another picture like it. He put down the sling. Tom lacked Dickinson's wit; she had hurled not a lethal rock, but only a pebble. But, in his lifetime, *Swimming* seemed only to have hit him, to have done him harm. It does so no more. The picture is so good, so inviting, that Eakins seems only to be saying come on in, the water's fine. And his sense of humor is back as well. His beloved setter, Harry, steals the show. You realize that the canine redhead will soon scramble up the rocks and, shake himself dry. A startled Talcott Williams, baking in the sun, will get a good spattering of fresh cold water.

Swimming is a great painting. Eakins, the artist, the man, has given us his pictorial sonnet.

The Pennsylvania Academy of the Fine Arts, c. 1890.
(Library Company of Philadelphia, Brenner Collection)

XIII

THE ACADEMY

AKINS' EFFORT IN *Swimming* to picture a world open to the sensuousness of art collided with the efforts of a crusader who sought to slam a door on just such licentiousness. In 1873, a moral crusader, as more than one encyclopedia categorizes Anthony Comstock, had persuaded Congress to pass anti-indecency legislation that President Grant, to his discredit, signed into law. The legislation also provided Comstock, a private citizen, with the unconstitutional authority to prosecute those who offended its provisions. In our time, in which there is so broad a license for expression, it is easy to laugh at Comstock, though, recently, others have taken up his work.

Comstock ushered in one of the most notorious of the intermittent periods in American history when sanctimonious censors have done great damage to freedom of expression and, in the doing, smashed careers. It was Anthony Comstock that wielded the mace this time. Eakins seems to have been oblivious of the threat, though it is highly unlikely that he would have trimmed his sails even if Comstock himself had come into his studio and attempted to do his repressive worst. A vengeful and eager seeker of pornography (broadly defined), Comstock can well be imagined ripping down the nude photos pinned to Eakins' studio walls.

Eakins may have paid a price for his lack of attention to the political world in which Comstock was at work. (Teaching at the Art Students' League in New York, he cannot have been oblivious of Comstock's actions. It would not have been out of character for Eakins to do a bit of parody, mocking Comstock's railing.) The more Comstock preached the evil of sin, the more the rest of the country felt the ripples and began seeing vice around every corner, including the artist's studio. Or elsewhere in the Pennsylvania Academy of the Fine Arts. Beulah Rhoades of Haddonfield, New Jersey, on her return from a photography exhibit there, wrote that she had noted a female nude in a "*very* prominent position"; because she thought this "unfavorable to the public morals," she made "a respectful . . . representation to the managers for its removal."[1]

One like-minded party had something to say about a particular studio. In the spring of 1882 a letter reached the chairman of the board of the academy, James L. Claghorn. Signed only R.S., it purported to be a letter from a mother greatly aggrieved by the threat to her daughter's morals. Every scholar who has considered the letter has assumed that it is the work of a mother, of a woman. I'm not so sure; there are notes struck that sound to me like the work of a man all too certain he knew the female mind.

"This is an age of progress I know & especially of great improvements in Arts & Sciences, & I acknowledge that every effort should be made & sustained with enthusiasm that promotes true Art. By *true Art* I mean the Art that ennobles & purifies the mind." And so it goes in this "appeal to you as a Christian gentleman, educated amidst the pure and holy teaching of our beloved Church. . . . This girl who has never seen her naked brothers was in a room in which both *male* & female figures stood . . . in their horrid nakedness." Worse, the "Professor [Eakins] walked around criticizing that nudity, as to her *roundness in this part*, and swell of muscles in another. . . . Do you wonder why so many art students are unbelievers even infidels?" Finally, the appeal is to the pocketbook: "Now Mr. Claghorn, does this pay?"[2]

Perhaps women were supposed to think this way; I'm not sure they did. You smell a male in the reasoning—"does this pay." Whatever the gender of the author, it laid the seed for some dirty work. President Claghorn and the other directors of the academy ordered this first such recorded attack on Eakins "filed"; but it was not forgotten.

It is not hard to imagine how eager a rebellious daughter of R.S. would have been to get safely into the depraved studio of Eakins, but just what was going on there? Actually, R.S. has told us a good deal about Eakins' teaching method. He did not simply have a model strike a classical pose nor was he content with a model in any pose. He wanted the students, the artists, to know the whole of the figure before them. He did go around the model and poke at the body to get the students to see its unique "roundness," to contemplate that particular person's musculature. Though a drawing was two-dimensional, Eakins was eager to have his students sense the figure in the round. If they were drawing an arm reaching across the torso, they should know how the back played into the motion.

Eakins was stretching taut the elastic of freedom. As secure as he was in his job, he was not invulnerable. He was at odds with the directors over a promise to double his salary that had not been kept. In fairness to the trustees, they had a truculent faculty member on their hands and Eakins had lost a loyal ally. In November 1883, Fairman Rogers, the sophisticated patron of the arts and admirer of Eakins' work, resigned as director of instruction and left the board of directors. In a note to Eakins, Rogers told the teacher he had championed that he was sure this would be unwelcome news. It was—and Eakins went to work to establish good relations with Rogers' replacement as director of instruction, Edward Coates, a man considerably less cosmopolitan than his predecessor.

Eakins' way of ingratiating himself drains *Swimming* of a certain innocence. Eakins was painting it for the boss. Edward Coates was building a house on a rural site on a millpond and wanted a picture of the area. He may not have known that it was to be populated in quite the way it was. Eakins presented the picture for inclusion in the fall 1885 exhibition at the Academy. Initially, Coates didn't get the point of the picture and it was proudly hung with his ownership acknowledged in the catalogue. Later in the fall he grew wary. He woke up to the fact that his millpond was full of naked men, which was more than he thought his living room could handle. On November 27, 1885, Coates wrote a long cautious letter gingerly making the suggestion that Eakins might allow him "to take something [else] of your work which you have on hand instead of the *Swimming* picture." Eakins, he added, could then send it to upcoming exhibits in New York, Chicago, and Boston.[3]

Eakins must have seen through Coates's muddling, but went along. Coates went home with another painting, one that was safely domestic but that also had an emotional meaning to Eakins: his father on his cello and Sue at the piano, are accompanying Margaret Harrison in full song, standing in a handsome dress, holding a score, *Singing a Pathetic Song*.

There were already other signals that trouble was brewing. The previous spring, Eakins had been scheduled to give a lecture on anatomy. The secretary of the academy was about to mail the customary invitations when Coates wrote, "I think it best to not issue *any* tickets for Mr. Eakins' lecture to press reporters."[4] What might their unpredictable professor say, let alone do, and, then, what might the wretches from the newspapers present for the rude gaze of public scrutiny? Word of Eakins' methods had reached the directors and they were uneasy.

Their worst fears were confirmed. Just after the New Year 1886 came the Affair of the Loincloth. In a life drawing class a male model wearing a loincloth stood before women students when Thomas Eakins, wanting to demonstrate movement in the groin, reached over and snatched the offending bit of cloth from the model. *Ecce homo*, Eakins was on his way out. Or so a too simple explanation goes. He had offended accepted morality. But much more was at stake.

If we can reach out visually to grasp his theme of liberation in *Swimming*, it is less easy to follow him into the studio and see that nakedness itself was a basic tenet of the creed. But for Eakins it was. He resolutely refused to have anything stand in the way of respect for the human body, all of it. His most ardent admirers still wish they could spare him the anguish this incident caused him and persuade him to see his own uncompromising stance contributed to his troubles.

Kathleen Foster, the ranking expert on Eakins, writes that the loin-cloth incident was "the defining moment in Eakins' teaching career. . . . From a distance, the forces of good (artistic freedom) and evil (Victorian repression) stand opposed like black and white."[5] In actuality, Thomas Eakins, the hero of a cause, was also Thomas Eakins of a personal tragedy. His flamboyant exercise of freedom, of even exultation, was capable of yielding to a dark streak of depression. Sylvan Schendler, an art critic and the author of one of the most penetrating studies of Eakins, called the removal of the loincloth "an immolation."[6] Had Eakins thrown himself on the pyre? Or had he made a brave stand for a principle he ardently believed in: the body, the whole body, was not an embarrassment; it was beautiful and should be matter-of-factly taken into account.

Not surprisingly, there are various versions of what actually did transpire. Whatever had transpired in the studio, it did not immediately cause Eakins to be fired. Initially, Coates, not eager to lose a good teacher, honored the commitment to Eakins that his professorship conferred. Seeking a compromise with his prominent, if difficult, instructor, he immediately ordered that male models wear a "band"; but before Eakins had a chance to defy him, he was summarily fired.

Before this compromise could be hammered out, a new variable had been introduced into the equation. Five of Eakins' students—Thomas Anschutz; Frank Stephens, who in 1885 had married Caddy, Eakins youngest sister; Frank's brother, Charles Stephens; James Kelly; and Colin Campbell Cooper—asked for a private meeting with the directors of the academy. The request was granted. Coates, though uneasy about Eakins, had, until now, tried to hold on to a distinguished teacher, one he did not want to lose. Now he gave up any attempt to keep Eakins. Why?

The five students can't have been simply going to repeat the story of the loincloth; everyone knew about that. Anschutz, who was the senior of Eakins' students and his assistant, running the dissection classes and helping out in the life drawing course, was accustomed to Eakins' unorthodox ways. He would not have been so shocked by the stripping of a model when there had been so much other nudity in the studio. Nor would a suggestion from the five that the school should be reorganized around new less controversial faculty have caused so swift a move as Coates was to make. The five must have dropped a bombshell.

Anschutz was second in command in the studio; the others had presumably enrolled in Eakins' courses out of eagerness to work with someone of his reputation. This virulent shift in their attitude represented either an actual aversion to the act they accused him of or an opportunistic embrace of scandal. Powerful circumstantial evidence points to the five's making an accusation that Eakins was an active homosexual. That Eakins was sexually attracted to males would not have been a surprise to all the directors; the damning indictment would have been that Eakins was described as having had a homosexual encounter, perhaps with a student. Given the prevailing ethos, even an encounter outside the academy would be deemed to impinge directly on the academy's reputation.

In the nineteenth century more than in the twentieth, as long as the dreaded word, whatever one was in use at the moment, was not mentioned, homosexuality could be tolerated. In fact, with more than a few people, homosexual acts, with no harm done, could still be tolerated. To others, homosexuality, explicitly known, was an inexcusable disgrace that stained not only the actor but the institution of which he was a part. It was this final point that weighed in with the directors. When the five young men confronted the board with some sort of evidence, the directors thought they could no longer look the other way. Publicly, officially, they could not countenance unmanly (or some similar euphemism) behavior by an instructor in the academy studios.

It appears that Eakins was too proud to mount a hypocritical defense of innocence; he was who he was. In a cold note, Coates, on February 6, asked for Eakins' resignation, to which, three days later, with an equally succinct note, Eakins complied.

Instantly, in the academy studios and soon all over Philadelphia, sides were taken. Tom and Sue saw members of their own families turn against them: Caddy and her husband, Frank Stephens, who were still living with Benjamin Eakins on Mt. Vernon Street; Sue's brother, William, and her sister, Elizabeth, to whom Sue pleaded to change her mind. Eakins' other students took passionate sides. On February 15, fifty-four of the male students (and one woman) petitioned to the directors to reconsider, saying that they had "perfect confidence in Mr. Eakins' competency as an instructor, and as an artist; and his personal relations with us have always been of the most pleasant character."[7]

Other students, hearing rumors of what the five had alleged, were confused. Some of the women who had been nude models turned on Eakins once he had become a publicly scandalous figure. The firing became a cause célèbre not only among the troubled students, but throughout the city. According him his honorific, a front-page story in the *Philadelphia Press* was headlined "Professor Eakins Resigns."

Some of Eakins' professional friends in the medical schools and the scientific departments of the University of Pennsylvania rallied to his side. Others dropped him; including Dr. Samuel Gross. Known by millions of admirers of *The Gross Clinic* who would otherwise never have heard of him as that man with the bloody scalpel, Gross published a two-volume autobiography in 1887, omitting no honor that came his way, including the placing of a marble bust in the Jefferson Medical College. However, neither Eakins nor his famous painting, also at the college, is mentioned.

On the other hand, in another branch of medical training, Horatio Wood, a distinguished professor of neurology at the University of Pennsylvania medical school, and S. Weir Mitchell, the country's best-known student of mental disorders, undertook to help their friend. They couldn't save the job for Eakins, but perhaps they could save him. They would have their chance later.

Some of his students moved more swiftly to rally to his cause. Within a week, all but twelve of the female students signed another petition asking the directors to reconsider. The directors didn't waiver; they released a formal statement: "The life school of the Academy is a benefaction established by the directors for the good of the students; and absolutely under the directors' control. It is their school and nobody else's."

This was a strange concept of the purpose of an art school. But the board soldiered on, acknowledging that some students would leave and correctly expecting some to stay. In a not quite seemly move, considering how the job opening had occurred, Thomas Anschutz was given Eakins' professorship; he was at the academy for the rest of his career. James Kelly was named his assistant in conducting the school. To Sylvan Schendler, this was scandalous. In his excellent essay on Eakins, he saw only self-serving on the part of Anschutz, who "had neither Eakins' intelligence nor moral sense, and so was able to stay at the Academy." What's more, in Schendler's scathing judgment, the man couldn't paint.[8]

The protests did not abate. Indeed they became so strenuous that the five accusers sent another petition to the directors, asking "most earnestly for an official statement from your Board to the effect that Mr. Eakins' dismissal was due to the abuse of authority and not to the malice of his personal and professional enemies."[9] Such twisted morality as this bears evil fruit. Colin Cooper was president of a student group that had been meeting informally to paint on their own. The group had nicely invited their teacher to be a member, only to rescind the invitation after the scandal broke. In an act of gratuitous ill spirit, Cooper wrote an icy letter dismissing Eakins as a member; Charles Stephens, who also sat on the overorganized club's executive committee, signed this arrogant dismissal letter as well. Another member, Frank Stephens, Eakins' brother-in-law, was not displaying excessive family loyalty.

Eakins' other brother-in-law, Will Crowell, thought he had a strategy that would help. He had a theory: was Stephens, having safely impregnated a wife, perhaps cloaking a homosexual venture of his own by accusing Eakins of one? Will Crowell thought so; he wrote Tom, "If Frank is using his [pregnant] wife's big belly as a rampire [rampart?] behind which, to wage such a warfare in security, the nature of his protection might at least be made public which would check his operations, if he is not stark mad," adding, "this your father and we could do."[10]

It may have been just as well that Will stayed out of Frank's gutter of accusation. But Tom wrote Fanny early in June that he could "no longer reconcile Frank's longer stay at home with the honor of the family,"[11] which meant that Caddy and her husband would have to leave 1729 Mt. Vernon Street. Benjamin Eakins agreed and took Tom's part, choosing a favored son over his youngest daughter and causing a wrenching breach in the close family. What the damage did to both children is hard to measure. Whether there was a residue of guilt that Tom shouldered we can only surmise.

Benjamin ordered the Stephenses out of the house. Tom and Sue would have preferred to stay at their place on Chestnut Street "where I have been very happy," but in time he came to realize that with the Stephenses gone, "Aunt Eliza should not be left alone neither should his father in his old days." Tom's fierce family loyalty was at work, which meant that Sue had years of care of elderly in-laws ahead of her. Eliza Cowperthwait was slipping into senility and Sue also would have to share Tom with his father, about to enter his seventies but no less strong-minded with Tom than he had always been. As for Caddy, her life was a troubled one—and brief. She died in childbirth three years later, at age 24.

Will Crowell's letter vehemently defending his old friend is interesting on two counts. It certainly demonstrated the extent of family loyalty to Tom. It also tells us that the subject of homosexuality was not alien to the society in which the Eakinses moved. Will, a sturdy family man and suburban farmer, was alert to the age-old strategem of those made uneasy by their own sexual orientation, who, seeking cover, attack those vulnerable to such a charge.

Whatever was the reason for Eakins to no longer protest, he paid a high price for stopping. The Pennsylvania Academy of the Fine Arts was an essential anchoring point for him. On one hand, it makes no sense that such a free spirit as he should be in the clutches of an institution so encrusted with a sense of its own importance as the first art school in the nation. In this respect Eakins was not a rebel. He had merged his life as a teacher and a painter into the academy. Eakins might have moved to New York; he taught at the Art Students' League and the National Academy of Design in New York and the Art Guild in Brooklyn, still an independent and vibrant city, but he was glued to Philadelphia.

Within ten days of learning that Eakins had been dismissed, his students had created a new place for him in the city. In temporary quarters on Walnut Street, they set up Philadelphia's Art Students League, modeled on the league in New York. In the announcement, they proudly listed Eakins as the only instructor. It was a warm invitation, but Eakins was too devastated to plunge into teaching with the vigor he had displayed at the academy.

Thomas Eakins would never get over the firing. It was not loyalty to an alma mater that held him: the Broad Street building was where he could teach. Artists assert that they teach in academe to put groceries on the table rather than out of a love of teaching. Not so with Eakins; as we have seen, he craved the companionship of his students. The academy's action threatened to drive a wedge into even those precious relationships.

But not if the students could help it. Forty of them, wearing an E on their hats, marched down Broad Street to the house on Chestnut where the Eakinses lived and Tom had his studio. Cheering and shouting his name, they stood outside in the street, but Thomas Eakins did not come out to greet them.

Cowboys in the Bad Lands, 1888. (The Anschutz Collection)

XIV

DAKOTA

THOMAS EAKINS' WORLD collapsed on top of him in 1886. His self-confidence vanished with his dismissal in February. In June, the torment had still not abated. As he wrote to his loyal sister Fanny, "For days I have been quite cast down being cut deliberately on the street by those who have every reason to know me."[1] He was immensely grateful to Fanny and to "Poppy," their pet name for their father. He had some hope that an affidavit designed for the academy directors and attesting to his excellent character, which Fanny and Will were prepared to sign, would help his cause, but in point of fact the document was so long and convoluted that it served no purpose. Eakins' own letters to Coates and to the parents of his students were also discursive, ranging in tone from defiant, to pleading, to explaining. The rupture at the academy could not be repaired.

The extraordinary display of loyalty by so many of his students, who demonstrated their affection by marching to his house, was more than matched by their eagerness to establish the Art Students League of Philadelphia. They imagined it as Eakins' own school, advertised it as such, and dreamed of its replacing the academy as the exciting place to study art. But they lacked the knowledge of how to organize a school, let alone how to pay the rent on studio space. Eakins' old friend from Paris days, Lucien Crépon, once more living in Philadelphia, who had some business sense, offered to help Tom out. The league did get started right after Eakins was fired. It lasted for six years, but it never really put its roots down: the key player in the enterprise never fully got it in focus. Eakins taught at the league, but more and more he was drawn to New York and Brooklyn, where he lectured, but had no studio in which he could teach. Instead of being fueled by the challenge of the new Art Students League in Philadelphia, he was humiliated by the cessation of his career at the academy. Eakins continued to teach, but never again did it give him the boost that it had previously.

Worse, he wasn't painting. There are almost no canvases for the eighteen months after his firing, nor any photographs. Eakins' friends were aware of his depression; they had only to look at his disconsolate appearance. William Marks, the engineering professor who had been on the committee supervising the Muybridge experiment with Eakins, invited him to accompany him, and his wife, and his daughter, to their summer place on Lake Champlain.[2] Tom stayed at this idyllic spot for two weeks, as June spilled into July. There was boating and good, if chilly, swimming, both among his favorite activities. He may have worked on a portrait he'd begun of Marks, one of only two paintings done that year.

Depression is the most elusive of maladies. In mid-nineteenth-century America, it had been termed melancholia; by the 1880s that romantic name was abandoned as the condition became recognized as a medical problem. Perhaps the most famous of the physicians who treated the problem was Tom's friend S. Weir Mitchell, who termed it "nervousness."[3] In his essay "Nervousness and Its Influence on Character," Mitchell presented case studies, most of them of women. He told of some of the most severe sufferers developing "hysteria," which he describes clinically. Mitchell does not omit men and his language fits Eakins' condition: "It is a common mistake to suppose that the well and the strong are not liable to onsets which cause nervousness. As a rule, they rarely suffer; but we are not neatly ballasted, some well people are nearer to the chance of being so overturned than it is pleasant to believe."[4]

After the debacle at the academy, Eakins certainly had reason to be depressed. As we have seen, he had struggled with the disease all his life. From Paris, Tom had taken note of a sentence of Benjamin's: "You have accused me of being either in the garret or the cellar."[5] Over his life-time Tom went through great swings in his sense of himself—when recognition belatedly came Eakins' way, he could walk into an exhibit of his work and get a standing reception one day and complain of being a failure the next.

Not the first, and surely not the last of America's charismatic doctors who have created cures that became fads, Mitchell advocated rest cure as a therapy for depression. His 1878 lecture, "On Extreme Measures in Therapeutics," met with skepticism by members of a medical audience in Baltimore. Even then, an admiring biographer noted, the word "'char-latan' had reached their ears."[6] Mitchell was undaunted and for good reason. By 1886 he had an honorary degree from Harvard and was elected president of Philadelphia's College of Physicians; in 1888 he was treated to a great banquet at the University of Bologna. His house in Philadelphia became a mecca for adoring women. His most popular medical books were *Fat and Blood* and *Wear and Tear*; his mantra for his women patients was "Rest, Diet, Massage." Following that advice and by being put to bed for months, the crusading feminist Charlotte Perkins Gilman was almost destroyed.

Mitchell's flamboyance and his misunderstanding of his female patients gave nineteenth-century neurology an undeserved bad name. It is easy to assume that no credible work was done in the field before Freud expounded his theories at the close of the century. Not so. And Thomas Eakins was the beneficiary of excellent assistance with the depression from which he was suffering. An 1863 graduate of the University of Pennsylvania School of Medicine, Horatio C. Wood in 1871 founded the first department of neurology in the country. Aware of Marks' intervention on Eakins' behalf, Wood sized up his friend's mal-ady and prescribed a cure.

Wood knew Eakins was both stubborn and independent and likely to resist treatment. Wood's strategy was to sit for a portrait; as Eakins was capturing the depth of Wood's psyche on canvas, Wood had his therapist's eye on Eakins. The portrait was not completed until 1890; Wood had his mental picture of Eakins much sooner. And he came up with a therapy. Shipping men out west to get them over whatever the east had done to them was a standard cure in the late nineteenth century and Mitchell concurred. The great outdoors on horseback was prescribed. Theodore Roosevelt famously rode off his asthma and possibly depression as well; Eakins' trip was designed to clear his head of Edward Coates.

Wood had all the ammunition; he owned a ranch in the Dakota Territory. Eakins traveled to his ranch for the summer of 1887, where the athlete in him would come to the fore. Wood's prescription was a good one. Eakins had the time of his life.

Tom, eager to give Sue a full account of his trip, exuberantly, if not accurately, drew a map on his letter of Sunday, July 31, 1887. On it, he placed the rivers, the Little Missouri running to meet the Yellowstone, which flowed into the Missouri. On the map was the Northern Pacific R.R. that had brought him to the town of Dickinson. There he had been met by Wood's manager Tripp, as his employer addressed him, in what is now the southwestern corner of North Dakota.

Waiting for lost luggage—Eakins' trunk came on the next train—they took in a trial at the courthouse. At issue was the sale of a steer by a man not its owner. Tom enjoyed the courtroom antics of the opposing attorneys. On Wednesday, with a horse Eakins had bought hitched to the wagon carrying the trunk, they set out to ride all night. A thunderstorm struck and they spent the night on a ranch along the way. There he met George Wood, Horatio's son; they became close friends.

One day soon after they reached the ranch, spotting antelope on a hill four hundred yards away, Eakins fired his gun and stirred up the ground close to the fleeing animal, passing muster as a hunter. He had intended to ride a bit each day to get used to the horse, but soon found himself riding long and hard through rattlesnake country. Fording the Little Missouri meant wet bedding. Eakins wrote his wife, "I did not catch any

Cowboy and Dog at the B-T Ranch, 1887.
(The J. Paul Getty Museum, Los Angeles)

cold sleeping in my wet clothes & wet bed. I had so many blankets that I kept warm and not uncomfortable. There were mosquitoes, but they don't seem to poison me here." All the eastern ailments, physical and psychic, were discarded; "the weather here is exceedingly beautiful."[7]

In another letter, dated August 28 but written over several days and full of enough lore for ten good western novels, Tom told Sue what he was learning—the farmers are called grangers (about as far as he got in grasping the Grange movement, a forerunner of the Populist party that attempted to deal with problems that farmers faced in the last decades of the nineteenth century); a little girl had a pet antelope that a cowboy had lassoed for her; game was hunted and berries collected to be preserved; a cattle owner rode seventy miles in search of cattle thought ready for a roundup (and didn't find them); he had seen two "Indian Squaws" out deer hunting; he was fascinated by the "cow-black-birds"

Eakins's Horse Billy and Two Crowell Children at Avondale, 1891.
(The Pennsylvania Academy of the Fine Arts)

that hitched a ride on galloping horses' backs; and on and on. He was already planning to bring back his horse and a pony for the nieces and nephews; there was not a hint of the troubles he had left behind.[8] He closed his next letter with, "How happy I shall be to see you again."[9]

On August 30, he replied to a letter from Sue that he had found a little doleful. At work while he was away, she was concerned about what she called a bad painting. "All painting is bad," he replied, "but yours is very good compared with other peoples'"—a limp and telling bit of commiseration. With Eakins away, Sue had gotten out her brushes and pigments; the tone of his reply suggests how hard it must have been for her to paint in his shadow. He, on the other hand, was full of beans. He has been told his horse "is the roughest on the ranch but I like his movement very well. . . . I do not get stiff or tired riding. I can ride all day and not feel it, but I get sleepy as soon as night comes and sleep right through the night."[10]

Crowell Family at Avondale, 1883. (Metropolitan Museum of Art, New York)

Early in October, riding on the train with a consignment of cattle for the Chicago stockyards, Eakins started his journey home. In a letter to his friend Johnny Wallace that December, he described his journey. On the Cumberland and Ohio Railroad instead of the Pennsylvania, he appears to be riding in the car with his two horses: "I was entirely comfortable, more so than in a sleeper. I could lie down or go back into the caboose or climb up on the top of my car to enjoy the scenery. I came through as pretty a country as ever I saw especially around Harper's Ferry that I passed soon after sunrise.

"The delay around Baltimore was probably fortunate for I arrived home in the middle of the night. If I had got in when school was out I fear I would have been as bad as a circus coming down Mt. Vernon Street with my broncho leading the mustang packed with my blankets and traps."[11] Tom was back home. The stay in Dakota had been wonderfully tonic, but once again a return home led Eakins to step back into his family routine. That night he climbed into the bathtub and then bed. A few days later, his father took the train to the suburb of Media to wait for him to arrive riding, Eakins recalled, "the broncho leading the pony," to deliver the horses to his sister and brother-in-law's Avondale farm. "At Kennett Square, six miles from the farm, we met Susie on horseback and all the little children and their father in the wagon coming out to meet us." Sue, a horsewoman, kept her horse at the farm and had gone on ahead to be there when the children saw their pony. The children, seven of the eventual ten Crowells, were the nieces and nephews so crucial to Eakins' happiness, yet ultimately the cause of so much heartbreak. Ella, the eldest, got on Sue's horse, the eldest boy, Ben, on the pony, Little Baldy, and "we scampered home like cowboys."[12]

Tom and Sue loved being with the Crowell children and spent a great deal of time at Avondale. The Eakins' camera was always with them and kept busy. There is a lilting quality to the best of the Eakinses' bucolic photographs of the children, often naked and playing in the brook.

Fanny and her husband, Will, the flock of children, the horses—all offered Eakins the best antidote to his depression. Philadelphia and its troubles were forty—four million—miles away.

Portrait of Walt Whitman, 1887–88.
(The Pennsylvania Academy of the Fine Arts)
See color plate 11.

XV

MICKLE STREET

I N THE SPRING of 1887, before he left for the Dakotas, Eakins met Walt Whitman. It was the beginning of perhaps the most remarkable friendship between an American poet and an American painter. Eakins had a rich group of intellectual friends, but Whitman was of a different order. His poetry spoke to Eakins' dream of freedom.

Whitman, having been in fragile health for twenty years, first came to Camden, New Jersey, the small industrial city across the Delaware River from Philadelphia, to stay with his brother George. When George moved twenty miles north to Burlington in 1884, Walt stayed behind, buying a small gray clapboard house at 328 Mickle Street, not far from the river.

Eakins was indebted to his good friend Talcott Williams for taking him to meet Whitman. Williams, just five years younger than Eakins, had recently been an Eakins student (and, in his midthirties, one of the models for *Swimming*). He became an editor of the *Philadelphia Press* in 1881. A general man about town and a notable conversationalist, he was a regular at Weir Mitchell's Saturday nights as well as gatherings at Whitman's

Mickle Street house in Camden. Like others of Eakins' friends, Williams was anxious to find new realms in which Eakins' troubles could be put aside. This trip to Camden made sense; Eakins knew and admired the poet's work. It was time he met the poet himself.

Eakins knew of the acolytes who came from all over the world to pay homage to the great poet, but paying homage was not his cup of tea. The guilt-by-association factor may have prevented Tom from seeking out the poet in years past. To visit Whitman was to invite gossip about his own sexuality. Now that Eakins' own sexuality was acknowledged by some, including Williams, Tom was curious to meet the most renowned of poets. When Williams and Eakins got to Mickle Street, Whitman found his new guest "careless, negligent, indifferent, quiet: you would not say retiring, but amounting to that."[1] Eakins' old shyness in unfamiliar social settings was at work. Whitman was also conscious that Eakins looked tired and troubled; up on gossip, Whitman knew what the good-looking, forty-two-year-old Eakins had been through at the academy. He invited him to come again.

On the next visit, Eakins was a new man. Back from Dakota, Eakins now often walked the short distance from his Chestnut Street studio, took the ferry over to Camden, and walked the few blocks to Mickle Street. Whitman, impressed with Eakins' appearance, commented, "You know Eakins the painter: he was sick, run down, out of sorts: he went right among the cowboys: herded, built up miraculously." Not only did Whitman note Eakins' physical condition, but he commented on what he thought Dakota had done for his painting: "it must have done much toward giving him or confirming his theory of painting: he has a sort of cowboy bronco method: he could not have got that wholly or even mainly in the studios of Paris—he needed the converting, confirming, uncompromising touch of the plains."[2] In short, Whitman recognized in the paintings of his new friend something like his own sense of place—his grasp of America—in his poetry.

Eakins must have taken some of his canvases to Whitman's house, but what ones and how many he does not tell us. *Swimming* would seem a perfect candidate, but there is no record from either man that it was shown to Whitman. The poet had himself once sought solace at a remote creek and pond called Timber Creek, and surely would have linked the picture to his own experience.[3] It would seem certain that some of the Dakota work made the trip to Mickle Street (and back; there is no record of Whitman having any of it on his walls).

Eakins' trips to Mickle Street became frequent. Told that his visitor was thought "uncouth, unchary, boorish," Whitman was asked if "Eakins wears well? Is he a good comrade?" The poet replied, simply, "He does . . . has a dry quiet manner that is very impressive to me." After further thought, Whitman added, "The parlor puts quite its own measure on social gifts: I should say Tom Eakins lacks them [as do I]: not that they are forgotten, despised, but that they enter secondarily. . . . Eakins might put it this way: first there is this thing to do, then this other thing, then maybe this third thing, or this fourth: this done . . . now the social graces."[4]

The two spoke the same language; as one acute observer put it, "the two men had common ground in their honest, in their anti-authoritarian impulses, and in their suspicion of official morality and official art."[5] The commonality of the two men was more than something negative. If Eakins had no political word to apply to that better world he sought, the poet surely did. J. M. Coetzee has spotted it. Whitman's "faith came out of a conviction, growing stronger as his interest in politics waned, that democracy was not one of the superficial inventions of the human reason but an aspect of the ever-developing human spirit, rooted in its eros: 'I cannot,' Whitman wrote, 'too often repeat that [democracy] is a word the real gist of which still sleeps. . . . It is a great word, whose history, I suppose, remains unwritten, because that history has yet to be enacted' "[6]

Coetzee explains, "Whitman's democracy is a civic religion energized by a broad erotic feeling that men have for women, and women for men, and women for women, but above all that men have for other men."[7] Eakins had been rebuffed when with *Swimming* he had tried to enact Whitman's desire with pigment on canvas. He regained it on Mickle Street. No longer uneasy in the presence of the poet, Eakins took command as the painter. He arrived, this time alone, carrying a stretched canvas and his working box. Whitman did not formally pose, but simply sat in his upstairs bedroom, by the window. Eakins, totally absorbed in the job at hand, went to work. He, Whitman noted with considerable amusement, "painted like a fury."[8] Two of the century's most extraordinary creative figures, two of the most American of American men, and two of its most outrageous, were face-to-face. The result was a painting by Eakins unlike any other.

Eakins at work was his usual thorough self. He began with a simple oil sketch of Whitman, who, like countless sitters, fell asleep while Eakins worked. The result is that this sketch of Whitman has a revealing, unself-conscious quality. For once, the Good Gray Poet has no chance to decide how to display himself; Whitman, for the moment, was indifferent to the effect he made. This was quite different from the studied pose of the famous engraving on the frontispiece of the first edition of Leaves of Grass, thirty-two years earlier.

Eakins, aware that his sitter was neither well nor young, came back for the usual many sittings he required to complete a work, but made them relatively brief. And frequent. A year later, Eakins was still at it; the two used the sittings in part to be together. As always, Eakins was painstakingly honest and meticulously accurate. Whitman had allowed himself, or rather chosen, to become a terrible mess, resisting both the barber's scissors and razor; he saw himself as a kind of Lear. But Eakins did not see Whitman as playing one of his parts, but as his friend, alert and amused sitting there enjoying the painter's company. Once, remembering being ill and unable to see visitors, Whitman said to his friend Horace Traubel, "You can imagine how I felt at the time I had to refuse Eakins. He is always welcome."[9]

In the final work, the poet is smiling and totally relaxed. Eakins was compulsive enough to laboriously re-create the lace on Whitman's feminine white collar, but otherwise, Tom allowed himself to be as relaxed as is his subject. Inaccurately, Whitman in a disingenuous bit of self-deprecation, chose to see himself as "a poor, old, blind, despised and dying king." The poet was closer to the mark when, in the same sen-

1. *Mrs. Edith Mahon*, 1904. Oil on canvas, 20⅝ x 16⅚ inches. Smith College Museum of Art, Northampton, Massachusetts. Purchased with the Drayton Hillyer Fund, SC 1931.2.

2. *The Writing Master (Portrait of Benjamin Eakins)*, 1882. Oil on canvas, 30 x 34 ¼ inches. The Metropolitan Museum of Art, New York. John Stewart Kennedy Fund, 1917.

3. *John Biglin in a Single Scull*, 1873–74. Oil on canvas, 24⁵/₁₆ x 16 inches. Yale University Art Gallery, New Haven, Connecticut. Whitney Collections of Sporting Art, given in memory of Harry Payne Whitney, BA. 1894, and Francis Payne Whitney, B.A. 1898, by Francis P. Garvan, B.A. 1897, M.A. (Hon.) 1922, June 2, 1932.

4. *Home Scene*, c. 1871. Oil on canvas, $21\frac{1}{16}$ x $18\frac{1}{16}$ inches. Brooklyn Museum of Art, New York. Gift of George A. Hearn, Frederick Loeser Art Fund, Dick S. Ramsay Fund, Gift of Charles A. Schiern.

5. *Rail Shooting* 1876.
Oil on canvas,
22 1/8 x 30 1/4 inches.
Yale University Art
Gallery. Bequest of
Stephen Carlton Clark,
B.A. 1903.

6. *Starting Out After Rail*, 1874. Oil on canvas mounted on Masonite, 24¼ x 19⅞ inches. Museum of Fine Arts, Boston. The Hayden Collection. Photograph © 2006 Museum of Fine Arts, Boston.

7. *The Gross Clinic*, 1875. Oil on canvas, 96 x 78½ inches. Jefferson Medical College, Thomas Jefferson University, Philadelphia.

8. *The Cello Player*, 1896. Oil on canvas, 64¼ x 48⅛ inches. The Pennsylvania Academy of the Fine Arts, Philadelphia. Joseph E. Temple Fund.

9. *The Artist's Wife and His Setter Dog*, 1884–89. Oil on canvas, 30 x 23 inches. The Metropolitan Museum of Art, New York, Fletcher Fund, 1923.

10. *Swimming*, 1884–85. Oil on canvas, 27 5/16 x 36 5/16 inches. Amon Carter Museum, Fort Worth, Texas. Purchased by the Friends of Art, Fort Worth Art Association, 1925; acquired by the Amon Carter Museum, 1990, from the Modern Art Museum of Fort Worth through grants and donations from the Amon G. Carter Foundation, the Sid W. Richardson Foundation, the Anne Burnett and Charles Tandy Foundation, Capital Cities/ABC Foundation, *Fort Worth Star-Telegram*, The R. D. and Joan Dale Hubbard Foundation, and the people of Fort Worth.

11. *Portrait of Walt Whitman*, 1887–88. Oil on canvas, 30⅛ x 24¼ inches. The Pennsylvania Academy of the Fine Arts, Philadelphia. General Fund.

12. *Baby at Play*, 1876. Oil on canvas, 32 1/4 x 48 inches. National Gallery of Art, John Hay Whitney Collection. Image © 2006 Board of Trustees, National Gallery of Art, Washington, D.C.

13. *Portrait of Professor Henry A. Rowland*, 1897. Oil on canvas, 80¼ x 54 inches. Addison Gallery of American Art, Phillips Academy, Andover, Massachusetts. Gift of Stephen C. Clark, Esq.

14. *Portrait of Mary Adeline Williams*, c. 1900. Oil on canvas, 24⅛ x 18⅛ inches. Philadelphia Museum of Art. Gift of Mrs. Thomas Eakins and Miss Mary Adeline Williams, 1929.

15. *The Thinker (Portrait of Louis N. Kenton)*, 1900. Oil on canvas, 82 x 42 inches. The Metropolitan Museum of Art, New York. John Stewart Kennedy Fund, 1917.

16. *Portrait of Amelia C. Van Buren*, c. 1891. Oil on canvas, 45 x 32 inches.
The Phillips Collection, Washington, D.C.

tence, he said it was "a portrait of power and realism."[10] "I never could get over," he told his friend Horace Traubel, "wondering that no one but two or three of us seem to like or even tolerate the Eakins picture of me. For myself I always say I am not only contented but gratified."[11]

Eakins cherished his private time with Whitman, preferring it to the frequent gatherings of admirers. The crowd around Whitman was largely gay and some of it effeminate in manner, which was never to Eakins' taste. On the other hand, he was completely at home in Whitman's house. Horace Traubel told of one occasion when William O'Donovan was working on a sculpture of Whitman: "Eakins [was] on a lounge in [the] front room, asleep, huddled up like a child. After a while he came sauntering out and entered our chat." Traubel said the sculptor and the painter were both "interesting men—Eakins more the genius, with cut free and original . . . dry humor, sententious—disposed to look at you and make his quiet, wise criticism and cease."[12]

Another frequent guest at Mickle Street was not male and Eakins knew and liked her. That winter, Eakins had met this engaging teenager, Weda Cook, at an Art Students League party. She had befriended her neighbor Whitman. Cook's spirited sense of humor made her a favorite of the aspiring young painters (and later one of Eakins' favorite models). She had grown up in Camden, thought when she first saw Whitman that she had seen Moses, and, a young girl not freighted with any undue awe, she often sang at gatherings at Whitman's house. Weda Cook's presence was a welcome antidote to some of the more obsequious guests.

Five years after the portrait was finished, Eakins and a group of Whitman's friends gathered to celebrate the poet's seventy-second birthday. There were many tributes to the great man. Talking about how he worked, Eakins told the gathering that when he went to work on his friend, "ordinary methods wouldn't do—that technique, rules and traditions would have to be thrown aside; that before all else, he was to be treated as a *man*, whatever became of what are commonly called the principles of art." It was a remarkable comment on his relationship to Whitman and, unwittingly, on the limitation in almost all of Eakins' work that precluded a lasting school of first-rate disciples. Tom was, indeed, bound by principles of disciplined art learned in Paris. His honesty carried all of his work beyond simple discipline, but, as an example of method, only the Whitman portrait pointed to the freedom in art that was to come in the century ahead.

Whitman was not concerned with what was to be, but with the unflinching honesty of Eakins' realism: "I never ... knew [but] one artist, and that's Tom Eakins, who could resist the temptation to see what they think ought to be, rather than what is."[13] Lit by light from the window, Whitman's face seems illuminated by that freedom of spirit to which both the poet and painter aspired. During their friendship, Eakins had been able to satisfy that desire as perhaps he had not in conversation with any other man. "Rabelaisian" was Whitman's word not only for the portrait that Eakins had done of him, but also for Eakins' conversation, which he relished. With this rich, unrestrained language, they could reach a frankness Eakins seldom allowed himself. The two men did not have to have sex for sexuality to be with them in the room. If Eakins knew the strength of *Song of Myself*, the appreciation was reciprocated. Whitman said of Eakins that he was more than "a painter—a force."[14]

It wasn't all Rabelais; there was a mutual fascination with photography, which Whitman saluted as a medium capable of that elusive thing, reality. On an early visit, Eakins brought his camera (not then a matter of tucking something in your pocket) and made the first of many photographs of Whitman. All of them are excellent photographs, and when he brought the handsome Sam Murray with him, surely not to Whitman's displeasure, the newcomer took some now famous photos of the poet as well.

Curious about Eakins' other work, Whitman was intrigued by the painter's *Gross Clinic*. Studying an engraving of the huge picture (he had never been to see it, although it was just across the river), he tried to imagine the red of the blood on Gross's hand. Whitman admired the raw power of the painting, which Eakins still regarded as his major work. Privately reciprocating, Eakins, not much at reciting poetry, left the declaiming to Whitman and went back to his copy of the *Leaves of Grass*

Thomas Eakins, *Walt Whitman*, c. 1891.
(Library of Congress)

with renewed wonder now that he knew its author. Both men had their share of rejection; Whitman could say of "the criticism of artists that Eakins was brutal, crude, bloody" only that the other artists "could not be expected to accept him—he inhabits another world."[15]

At Whitman's 1891 large birthday party, the poet asked the painter, "Haven't you something to say to us, Eakins?" Tom replied, "I am not a speaker," to which Whitman said, "So much the better." So Eakins had his say: "I some years ago . . . painted a picture of Mr. Whitman. I began in the usual ways but soon found that the ordinary methods wouldn't do—that technique, rules and traditions would have to be thrown aside; that before all else, he was to be treated as a *man*."[16]

On March 26, 1892, Walt Whitman died. Eakins, Murray, and two assistants made Whitman's death mask; Tom placing the wax on his friend's cold face himself. He was one of a throng of pallbearers, one still young and strong enough to escape the status, of "honorary" and to bear the weight of his comrade as they carried him to the gaudy mausoleum that Whitman, perversely, had had constructed. But Eakins' private mourning was lost to us in what became the circus of the vast crowd along the way out of Camden to the cemetery on the Haddonfield road. Unlike the solemnity of standard nineteenth-century funerals, Whitman's turned into a raucous celebration. Eakins led the mourning artists in the crowd back to Philadelphia to his Chestnut Street studio, where he had his share of drinks. At one point, Tom picked up Weda Cook and placed her on a table, where she sang a rousing irreverent musical version of "O Captain! My Captain."[17]

Sober but not solemn, the portrait was Eakins' matchless memory of the poet. Over the years, Eakins had continued to visit his friend whose health, despite several seeming recoveries, was deteriorating. Now the man was gone whose work had expressed the reality of life rather than its conventional surfaces, who had dared sing openly of the sexuality that Eakins, bedeviled, had kept silent about in public. The painter had finally, in the privacy of Whitman's room, been able to sing, and the portrait was his song.

Baby at Play, 1876. (National Gallery of Art)
See color plate 12.

XVI

ELLA

E LLA CROWELL, TWENTY-FOUR, with none of her family present, reached into the fireplace of the family farmhouse, put a bullet in the rifle stored to the side of the chimney, went upstairs to a bedroom, put the end of the barrel in her mouth, and with a stick carefully chosen and shaped, pressed the trigger.[1] The next day, July 2, 1897, the deputy coroner, Lewis W. Lipp, and Dr. U. G. Gifford drove out to investigate the killing. In the county coroner's docket, they gave the details, ruled the death a suicide, and "exonerated the family from all blame."[2] On the seventh, Will and Fanny Crowell saw their daughter's casket lowered into the soil of the farm.

Ella had been the subject of one of Eakins' loveliest paintings, *Baby at Play,* in which a toddler plays with toys in the sunlit backyard of 1729 Mt. Vernon Street. The art historian Jules Prown sees the picture as of "a human being at the beginning of the adventure of life."[3] In it, a child has put aside a doll to push a toy horse and wagon, while also playing with blocks. At fourteen, Ella had proudly ridden a horse from the

Avondale farm to Media to meet her uncle back from Dakota—with his new horse and a pony for Ella's six little brothers and sisters.

As she grew older, Ella showed signs of mental illness. On one occasion, denied permission to ride into the city, she "got on her horse and rode it at so furious a rate around the farm that the beast was exhausted, then betaking herself to the meadow stream, remained in swimming until exhausting herself."[4]

Tom and Sue were so close to Will and Fanny that it was likely that they were consulted about Ella's condition. Tom, wanting to help, invited her and her sister Margaret to move to Philadelphia and study with him. Very young—Ella was only seventeen and Margaret fourteen—they arrived in town to stay with Tom and Sue. Margaret showed some talent at drawing; Ella was simply restless. As she grew older, she gave up the study of art and entered nurses' training at the Presbyterian hospital. Once, she is said to have given a patient an overdose of medication that nearly killed her. Ella took the same dose and nearly died.[5]

By then, the family realized they were confronting "mental instability," as it was delicately termed. How serious they determined it to be is not clear. Ella's haunted face in a photograph taken probably in 1897 reveals how ravaging her insanity had become. In August, 1896, the Crowells had taken the drastic step of committing Ella to the Norristown Asylum for the Insane. Nothing is known about the treatment that she was given; all we know is that the coroner's report of her death said simply that she had recently been "parolled."

While home from the asylum, Ella told her parents of happenings at Mt. Vernon Street. Believing her, Fanny and Will wrote to Tom and Sue that this "unparalleled provocation" had caused Ella's illness. No details were given. Receiving the letter, Sue was furious. Instead of suggesting that she and Tom come to Avondale to discuss the parents' overwrought response to a family calamity, Sue wrote to the Crowells saying their attitude toward Tom was "detestable and outrageous" and that the girls were no longer welcome. Margaret was still in the city; "that Ella, if she recovers will prefer to come here again decided me to write."[6]

Thomas Eakins, *Ella Crowell*, 1897.
(The Pennsylvania Academy of the Fine Arts)

Then came Ella's death. A life was lost and a whirlpool of grieving engulfed the two families. Suicide is a lonely path. Those who embrace it refuse any companions. To silence the demons the world has let loose on them, the determined travelers go their inexorable way to their terrible sanctuary. They call down the gods to wreak vengeance on those they blame, rightly or wrongly—even indiscriminately—for the act

they take. In this case, intentionally or not, Ella Crowell inflicted a terrible punishment on both her parents, on her siblings, and on Sue and
Tom Eakins.

The damage done was immense. The death tore in two what had
been one almost inseparable extended family. Always welcomed at
Avondale by Will Crowell and Fanny, Eakins was now banned. It was a
lacerating blow. The time with the Crowell children was precious to Sue
and Tom; the farm itself, and its lovely surroundings had long been an
essential component of Tom's being. The Crowells' accusation was
unequivocal and instantaneous. Their daughter's death was Thomas's
fault. Susan Eakins responded with equal firmness, rejecting any guilt on
her husband's part.

Assigning blame for a suicide is a fruitless task. The undeniable mental illness that Ella suffered would seem to preclude any single cause.
Tom may have done something untoward, an action that his sister and
brother-in-law magnified and grasped at. Where there is this much
smoke, you suspect fire. And yet blame seems out of order. If the parents
could never be forgiving, and neither could a distraught Margaret, the
younger Crowell children did not harbor negative feelings about their
uncle Tom for long. Years later, the recollections of Jim, the youngest,
seemed entirely pleasant. Jim told mainly of family musicals—
sometimes transferred to the Eakins house in town. "Although he did
not play an instrument," Jim recalled, "he shared his wife's and sister
Frances's deep feeling for music: he sometimes wept when he heard passages from Brahms and Beethoven." Jim offered no explanation for the
banning of Tom from Avondale,[7] but his reminiscence suggests how
strong had been the tie between the two families.

The suicide foreclosed any chance to restore that affection.[8] The
breach between Avondale and Mt. Vernon Street was never healed. For
Tom, to be barred from Avondale was to lose half his family, his only
children, a sister, a friend. A decade earlier he had lost the millpond; now
the loss of the farm was like the amputation of a limb. He cannot have
been callous enough to brush such a loss aside, but he seemed to have
done just that.

Leaving Sue behind to do battle for his honor with his sister Fanny, Tom went off to Maine, and as lively a time as he ever had working on a painting. The family tragedy seemed not to have affected Eakins' work as an artist—work that had resumed so well after his return from the west—unless it deepened his sense of the sadness he saw in women he painted. Friends of the Eakinses and particularly of the Crowells must have thought his abrupt departure to the popular summer resort on Mount Desert Island strange. Sue saw it as essential if he were not to crack. In everything he did at this lovely vacation spot, in all of his long letters home to Sue, he gave not a sign of any emotion roused by Ella and the devastation her suicide had left in its wake. He left Philadelphia shrouded in an amnesia summoned to save his sanity.

Portrait of Professor Henry A. Rowland, 1897.
(Addison Gallery of American Art)
See color plate 13.

XVII

MOUNT DESERT

THE PREVIOUS WINTER, Eakins had persuaded another scientist, Henry A. Rowland, to sit for a portrait. Rowland, a founding faculty member of the prominent research institution the Johns Hopkins University in Baltimore, was one of the country's leading scientists. Known for his research on magnetism, he had laid the groundwork for the design of the transformer, which had many important applications, among them the generation and transmission of electric energy at high voltage. (Henry Adams gave the layman an indelible image of such power when, at the Paris Exposition in 1900, he encountered his "Dynamo," a vast throbbing mass of parts whose energy he declared the "symbol of infinity.")[1]

Most relevant to Eakins' portrait of Rowland was the physicist's work on light. As a scientist explains, "Colors are easily seen when light passes through a glass prism, but this does not permit precise measurement of each emitted wavelength. To do so requires what is called a diffraction grating, a series of fine, densely packed scratches on a glass surface. When light passes through the grating a series of bright and dark lines are seen,

looking like a bar code, and the distances between these lines corre-
spond to the wavelengths. Rowland's contribution was to create an
'engine,' as the device was termed, that would enable making a diffraction grating on a curved, rather than flat, surface, a major improvement
in the analysis of the chemical makeup of things by means of the light
they emit when heated to incandescence."[2] The engine, in vivid color,
rests in Rowland's hand in the completed painting.

Busy in his laboratory during the school year, Rowland found it hard
to be available to sit for a formal portrait and made the familiar academic's mistake of thinking that during the summer he would have plenty
of free time. He invited Eakins to come to his summer place at Seal
Harbor, a lovely spot on Mount Desert Island. Once again a scientist, as
Wood, the neurologist was, provided an opportunity at exactly the right
moment for Eakins to regain his emotional bearings away from
Philadelphia.

Thomas Eakins never had more fun painting a portrait. So much fun
that it is a wonder that the picture progressed at all. The culprit: a boat,
and a good one. The time, August; the delinquents, two middle-aged
maniac sailors who couldn't resist the temptation of such a fine stretch
of water along a beautiful coastline.

Eakins shipped his brushes and paints and, on July 20, 1897, set off by
train for Maine. The Bar Harbor Express left Philadelphia for Hoboken,
where the passengers took the ferry to New York City. There Eakins
boarded a second train to continue his comfortable course to Maine.
Arriving at Hancock Point, Eakins took the steamer to Bar Harbor, and,
at the end of a long day, a carriage the short distance to the Glen Cove
Hotel in Seal Harbor. In his first letter to Sue, this one written "before
breakfast" the day after his arrival, he complained that one couldn't get
the morning meal at 6 a.m., his bicycle hadn't yet arrived—and he had
missed his early morning ride.[3]

Persevering until eight—and a good breakfast—Eakins set off to walk
"about two squares," as he put it in good Philadelphia fashion, to the
Rowland's house on Ox Hill.[4] And wonderful that house was. Designed
by Isaac Green, a master of the shingle style, it had just been completed

the year before. Eakins commandeered a room in spacious, airy Craigstone, as the house was grandly named, to use as his studio. After meeting the professor's wife and two children, he sat Rowland down and did a "pretty satisfactory" sketch. Eakins acquiesced to Mrs. Rowland's request that her husband be done in "dark clothes," but in a letter home he added, "I shall be the final judge of what I want." And in a portent of things to come, reported laconically that after lunch he "went sailing with Rowland all the afternoon."[5]

The sailor in Maine was a different man from the Baltimore scientist, known for his severity in the laboratory. He asked Eakins to be sure not to give his face a sailor's sunburn, lest his scholarly reputation be brought into question. Unfortunately, the artist complied. The *Portrait of Professor Henry A. Rowland* is a great painting, but what if Eakins had painted Rowland in that boat? He could have shown an athlete, ruddy and strong, and reclaimed for both of them the freedom Eakins displayed in his early paintings of men out sailing. Instead, in the finished picture Rowland is shown in a suit with proper laboratory pallor. In fact, Rowland was the greater of the two truants; Eakins had some sense that there was work to be done. He "was at the forehead" one morning when a "thunderstorm came down fortunately from the mountains at lunch time and so we could not go sailing, so Rowland sat a while for me in the afternoon." But Eakins does not seem to have tried too strenuously to discipline his sitter, and he was not immune from an enthusiasm of his own.[6] One day, when there was no wind, the ardent cyclist got the renowned physicist on a bicycle. "I insisted on teaching him to ride." After his third lesson, "he rode a quarter of a mile and almost straight."[7]

On one expedition, they stopped at a carpentry shop for sticks for a kite that they set to constructing with "scientific" attention to strain factors. Science failed them. The "abomination" would not fly.[8] When he got back to Philadelphia, Eakins sent Rowland "two little Japanese kites," which, Rowland reported, "flew like birds—whenever they see a tree they dive for it . . . and perch in its branches."[9] The business of the kites suggests that Rowland and Eakins shared a sense of the symmetry of science and art. They could laugh at themselves and their aerody-namic failure, but they knew the beauty of things. "A yacht is beautiful & shapely," wrote Eakins, reflecting on a kite in flight, "and so are all good things, flowers, axe handles, the tools of workmen, but above all the living animal forms."[10]

Thomas Eakins liked being in the company of a working scientist: "There is no one in the world who holds a higher position in science than Rowland." And the painter could hold his own in their conversa-tions, which were not all about the spectra. Sailing got its share. On August 9, the harbor was full of steam yachts just completing a race: "The whole fleet will sail this morning for Bar Harbor nine miles north, so no painting today. . . . Rowland couldn't pose if he tried. He is a big bad boy."[11] The pot calling the kettle black. In fact, Eakins was becoming seduced by all around him. Why go to France, when you can be on Mount Desert? he asked in one letter.

Summer life at Seal Harbor stimulated Eakins to uncharacteristic ambition. He was almost driven to hunting among the grandees for sub-jects to paint. Learning that William Thomas, Baron Kelvin, was coming to the island on his way to Toronto for the British Association of Science meeting and would be staying with the Rowlands or with the president of Johns Hopkins, Daniel Coit Gilman, in Northeast Harbor, Eakins offered to do Kelvin's portrait and give it to the university. Unfortunately, nothing came of this, but the absence of another paint-ing assignment meant more time for sailing. Any excuse would do: "Yesterday afternoon we sailed over to South West Harbor to buy 3 cups and saucers." That emergency taken care of, they "got back at 6 'o'clock just in time to avoid a sudden fog that shut everything from view." The fog lifted the next morning and with a "strong northeaster blowing," Rowland wanted to sail. "We took in one reef and went way out to sea." When the artist confessed that he had been horribly seasick on his first trip to Europe, the scientist told him that "I would not get sea sick in so small a boat and he was right."[12]

Tom shared all of this with Sue, and waited impatiently for her letters—the bellboy at the hotel was instructed to wake him if one came in late in the evening. His letters were chatty—how are the fish, has "brother turtle laid more eggs"—and full of Mt. Vernon Street concerns—Aunt Eliza's precarious health worried them—and toward the end of his stay, particularly affectionate: "I am so sorry you feel low spirited and wish ever so much I could see you. It won't be very long." But, even at that moment, his attention returned to his painting: "I am going over the head again. You know I had finished it all in an hour & a half. It was pretty strong in a way but coarse. A head can hardly be gone over in that time."[13]

Eakins' letters give us a glimpse of how the artist worked. Sailing or no, he did an enormous amount of work in the brief weeks that he was at Seal Harbor. Tom did not date his letters and it is hard to be sure how much time elapsed between them. Within a week, after Rowland had sat for only a few hours, Eakins reported that a second, probably an oil, sketch was complete "of a good characteristic pose." His canvas was stretched, an undercoat of paint applied, and the perspective outlined. He was optimistic that it would be a good painting, expecting it to be as good as his study of Rudolph Hennig, the distinguished musician pictured in *The Cello Player*. Of the Rowland portrait, he said, "I shall try to finish it without getting tired or stale." On Saturday (probably July 31) he reported: "I got my canvas all covered, . . . and had another sitting making about 4 hours in all."[14] The next day, working alone, he "got more paint on to thin parts & straightened up drawing of chair,"[15] and left the canvas to dry a bit.

In the week following, new pigments arrived and he was able to reach "the secondary perspective pretty well. The green is not at all the one I sent for but it appears to do very well."[16] The painting progressed meticulously; he worked on the forehead alone for hours and, another day when weather prevented their afternoon sail, he "finished the other hand: not a great deal to be sure for you only see the tips of his fingers but it was that much nearer to home. Today I shall go over the chin and jaw."[17] As Eakins began to assemble the whole of him, Rowland, who had not expected much to begin with, became intrigued with what his new friend was accomplishing.

Determinedly, Eakins wrote to Sue, "Next week I shall be home (finished)." He had planned to paint Rowland only, leaving the completion of the significant items in Rowland's laboratory room for his return to Philadelphia; he already knew he wanted to include Rowland's "machine," the diffraction grating "engine," and to show Rowland's assistant at work in the back shadows of the painting.[18]

Eakins had thought of stopping in Portland on his way home and heading out to Prout's Neck to meet Winslow Homer, but decided against it. It would have been a long detour and he was uneasy about disturbing the painter, with whom he had much in common. There is no record that the two met, or even corresponded. If his plans worked out, Eakins did stop in Boston to see some Sargents that were on exhibit.[19]

Home in Philadelphia, Eakins buckled down and finished the painting. Rowland, sedate, pince-nez on his formidable nose, his "engine" on the table behind him, wears his brown suit, while the assistant and the equipment on which he is working are depicted in tan tones. But there is, for Eakins, a daring touch. In the physicist's hand is a palm-sized instrument recording in brilliant color the spectrum so emblematic of Rowland's work. Tom gave the portrait an elaborate frame, a motif of some of the physicist's equations carved into the broad wooden surface. The equations for the diffraction grating on two plane surfaces are in the frame's top and bottom.

Eakins had done well by his summer friend, but the memories of the days they worked—and played—together became bittersweet. The fate of the picture, and of its subject, added to the cumulative sadness with which Eakins was freighted in the last decades of his life. By that summer, Rowland, so vigorous, had already been diagnosed as a diabetic. Less than four years later, at age fifty-three, Rowland died, not heroically lost in a North Atlantic storm, but at home, in Baltimore. Their friendship had been brief, but seldom had Eakins enjoyed one more.

Rowland's family declined to purchase the picture. Eakins exhibited the canvas in several shows, but it did not sell. Through a friend, it was offered in 1908 to Johns Hopkins, the university to which Rowland had brought so much honor; President Ira Remsen replied, "I wish we owned it but we have one life-sized portrait of Professor Rowland, and I do not know where we could go to secure the funds to buy another."[20] Rowland's grand portrait joined the other canvases stacked against the wall at 1729 Mt. Vernon Street. It was there when Eakins died in 1916.

It was finally sold, in 1929, to a collector, Stephen C. Clark. In 1931, Clark gave it to Phillips Andover Academy for its astonishingly good art collection. At first blush, it seems to be hanging on the wrong wall, that of a privileged preparatory school. No committed research scholar gets to confront a forebear as he daily makes his way into a Johns Hopkins laboratory. But perhaps in Andover's Addison Gallery, Rowland occasionally catches the quick eye of a would-be physicist—or painter. Perhaps it is as it should be that the painting is there. The school's teenage students, boys and girls still, have much in common with Tom Eakins and Henry Rowland on their boat in the summer of 1897. Luckily, they don't yet carry the emotional freight that Eakins then did.

Samuel Murray, 1889. (Cedarhurst Center for the Arts)

XVIII

SAMUEL MURRAY

AKINS' WORK WAS his first concern, but it was done in a narrower Philadelphia. There was no more relaxing out at the Avondale farm; he was deprived of the companionship of Ella's brothers and sisters and denied, as well, both his horse and the comfort and ease of the country. The house on Mt. Vernon Street itself was diminished. Death was subtracting from the once large embracing ledger of family. It had begun long ago, in 1872 when Tom's mother died, again in 1882 with his sister Margaret's death, and, scarcely less telling than the human losses, his dog Harry, his great friend, died in 1894. Harry had been party to some of Eakins' most revealing paintings; he is at Susan's feet in the wedding picture and in the water in *Swimming*.

Eakins' aunt Eliza Cowperthwait died in January 1898, soon after he returned from Maine. Deaf, nearly blind, and senile, she had been a difficult care at the end, but for decades she had been part of the household and was Tom's last immediate link to his mother's Cowperthwait family. Finally, an even more critical loss: in December 1899, Benjamin

Addie Williams, c. 1899. (The Pennsylvania Academy of the Fine Arts)

Eakins, the paterfamilias who had been so steadfast in his support of his son Tom, was gone.

Benjamin's house had been a family's center; Susan always referred to it as "Mr. Eakins' house." It had been home to so many rich family transactions, from bonding with new in-laws to too many wrenchings apart

Portrait of Mary Adeline Williams, c. 1900. (Philadelphia Museum of Art)
See color plate 14.

of the family; now it was empty of all but one Eakins. Tom now had his studio on the third floor, his ragtag menagerie of creatures on the first, but more and more it was Susan's house that gave life grounding.

One new resident did grace 1729 Mt. Vernon Street. In 1899 Mary

Adeline Williams moved in with the Eakinses. The Williamses, neighbors of the Fish House in rural New Jersey, had been friends of the Eakinses for decades; Addie, with something of a lifelong crush on Tom, had in her teens sent the lively young man, who was then in Paris, a picture of herself and her infant sister, Annie. She had been sent to school in Philadelphia where she was friends with Margaret Eakins. When Addie's widowed father remarried, she got a job in Wanamaker's department store sewing blouses for a pittance.[1] In her fifties, she was a familiar nineteenth-century figure—an unmarried female with no profession.

Addie played the piano well, but not professionally, had no income beyond her small salary, and, getting older, was wholly dependent on the kindness of whatever family could provide safe harbor. She found it with Tom and Susan, with whom she soon became inextricably attached. The year she moved in, Susan reports, "Tom, Mr. Eakins and Addie Williams and I took the train to Egg Harbor by train and then on bicycles to Atlantic City."[2] (This was one of Benjamin Eakins' last outings; he died that December.) Addie was one of the family. Outsiders referred to her as companion to Susan, the polite term for a woman in her position. The two paintings Tom did of her when she lived with them are among his best portraits, brutally frank and, at the same time, sympathetically honest. There is no glamour in either; instead, he has empowered Addie with dignity.

More than ever Eakins valued his friendship with Samuel Murray. The two men loved each other and the companionship was crucial to them both. A remarkable picture of the pair with the sculptor William R. O'Donovan, taken by Susan Eakins, shows three artists relaxing in Eakins' Chestnut Street studio in 1891 or 1892. The photograph tells more about the friendship, and Eakins' wife's understanding of it, than any of the many other images of the two.

Murray, born in 1869, was the eleventh child of a family that had emigrated from Cork, Ireland. Sam's father was a stonecutter at Woodlands Cemetery; in a nice leap, the son became a sculptor. As a teenager he joined the Art Students League and studied with Eakins. He soon became an assistant to his instructor, helping with *The Agnew*

Susan Macdowell Eakins, *Samuel Murray, Eakins, and William O'Donovan in Eakins's Chesnut Street Studio*, c. 1891–92.
(The Pennsylvania Academy of the Fine Arts)

Clinic. Murray recalled Eakins sitting cross-legged on the floor working on the picture and later made a sculpture of the artist in that position.[3]

Sculpture, rather than painting, was Murray's medium; much of his work is now in the Hirshhorn Museum in Washington. The two men shared the Chestnut Street studio and became inseparable. Tom took him to meet Whitman, and as we have seen, the photographs Murray took of the poet became renowned. Lloyd Goodrich, always cautious in his assessments of Eakins' sexual relationships, told in the early 1930s of a then rather deaf Murray always speaking of Eakins "with understanding and love."[4] "Love" is a word often sneaking into descriptions of the relationship of the two men. Clothed or naked, Murray was dazzlingly handsome and Eakins, into his sixties, was still a striking man. Even those writers who believe that the men slept together tend to downplay the sexual act, equating it to bike rides or fishing expeditions. But, to be true to the Eakins story, the possibility has to be taken into account.

A classic pose for a model in an artist's studio is a nude woman reclining on the floor visible from the rear, with posterior in full view. There is one such photograph of a female model in Eakins' studio, but there is another of Eakins himself in exactly the same pose. This image and many of the other photographs of Eakins naked led the twentieth-century composer Ned Rorem to write, regretfully, "I can never meet and sniff and love, say, Thomas Eakins. Not his painting, but the finite trembling man. Long for his flesh, which was gone before I was born."[5] We have no nineteenth-century diary as frank as the composer's; we can only conjecture, as Rorem has, that Eakins found great satisfaction and serenity in such sexual fulfillment. On the other hand, it almost certainly delivered deep depression when he denied himself of it.

Tom and Sam were inseparable throughout the 1890s. Out of the studio, out of the house, Eakins and Murray found yet another sport: boxing. One sportswriter estimated Tom saw three hundred rounds of fighting. He was an eager fan, writhing around in his seat and jumping to his feet so energetically that once a man in the adjacent seat protested.[6] Sam, on the other side of him, wasn't surprised. Back in the studio, Eakins brought his new sport to canvas. He painted three huge images of boxers: *Between Rounds*, with his favorite, Billy Smith, being fanned by his trainer; *Taking the Count*, of two other boxers, the loser being counted out and the victor standing over him; and *Salutat*, with Billy raising his victorious arm to the crowd. The arena in all three paintings—with banners advertising other entertainments, rows and rows of spectators, all with differentiated faces—offers a wonderful period piece; you can almost smell the place.

At first glance, it would appear that Eakins was back to the sports paintings of his early career. Much as he had done with Max Schmitt sitting in his scull, Tom painted Billy Smith as someone more than a boxer. As in his great pictures of the amphitheaters of *The Gross Clinic* and *The Agnew Clinic*, in each of the boxing pictures, Eakins masterfully

Salutat, 1898. (Addison Gallery of American Art)

handled the many faces in the crowd watching the action. But there is something different in these paintings. Instead of being out on the Delaware River in sparkling light, sailing with carefree friends, we are inside in a smoke-filled arena. The Biglin brothers displayed their prowess with no competitor in sight to vanquish, but in Eakins' paint-

ings of Billy Smith, he is the winning boxer, looking down on his oppo-
nent taking the count. The audience of men (and apparently only one
woman) is depicted in a historically accurate rendering of the noisy
crowd, painted with no less precision than the medical students looking
down at the operation underway in the surgical amphitheaters of Dr.
Gross and Dr. Agnew. But, instead of medical students being instructed
by an operation designed to cure, here we encounter a crowd lusting
after blood and violence. Even the handling of Smith's body, pale almost
to a silver gray, contrasts with the golden bodies in *Swimming*.

Instead of innocence regained, there is a sense of its irretrievable loss
in the boxing paintings. These three seem to speak of hope abandoned,
of a capitulation to what had happened to Eakins' world. There is no
longer the smell of mown spring hay at Avondale, only the sweat and
smoke of the closed-in arena. Thomas Eakins was seeking pleasure out
of weary desperation, not in affirmation. He is, in these pictures, as
Melville was when he left Billy Budd in that bottom drawer. Walt
Whitman was dead and soon, so would be their century, which had
once held such promise.

It was not all shades of dark. Eakins and Sam found other ways to be
together, including the cycling they both loved. On Sundays they would
roam the streets and paths of Philadelphia's huge 8000-acre Fairmount
Park. There were vast fields then and wonderful trees; there was also the
predictable pretentious monument to Civil War heroes and nearby a
domed building left over from the Centennial Exposition.

Not far from the park, Thomas Eakins found sanctuary in an unex-
pected place, the St. Charles Seminary. Eakins was a nonbeliever, or at
least a freethinker, but here, away from the world of studios and the
smell of linseed oil and pigments, the rough and tumble of boxing are-
nas, Eakins found respite in the neighborhood of Overbrook, the seminary's site. Named for the sixteenth-century cardinal of Milan, Charles
Borromeo, a leader in the Counter-Reformation whose means of attack
was reform of a lax and corrupt clergy, the American seminary was a
distinguished center for Catholic learning—and foreign territory for
someone living in starchy, Protestant Philadelphia.

Saint Charles Borromeo Seminary.
(Photograph by Eliza McFeely)

If this was a world alien to Thomas Eakins, it was not to Sam Murray, who was an Irishman and a Catholic. On Sundays Tom and Sam often made Overbrook the goal of their bicycle pilgrimages. It was ideal cycling country for the two energetic men. Leaving the park, it was only a short way to the seminary. For a non-Catholic, a seminary can conjure up strange, formidable medieval images. It took someone born in faith, to be comfortable walking in the door, and Sam Murray, one of whose sisters was a Sister of Mercy, was one. He escorted Eakins safely through the door.

The seminary, founded in 1832, had moved to Overbrook in 1871 and by 1900 was housed in an imposing symmetrical three-story stone building. A handsome chapel lay at the building's center on the first floor; it was surrounded by classrooms. The faculty lived on the second floor, the seminarians on the third.

From his first visit on, Tom was happy to make this the goal on their various winding routes through the park lying on either side of the Schuylkill River. Sunday afternoon, after mass, was a relaxed time for the nearly one hundred students of the seminary and more than a dozen faculty members. The priests who taught there had been trained largely in Europe and were serious scholars with whom Eakins could hold his own. It is difficult to imagine that religion did not raise its head in the conversation on those Sundays as they sat out on the spacious grounds under the shade of copper beech.

He was an "agnostic," Eakins said to one inquiring priest, who was untroubled by his answer. It was the companionship of this male community that drew Eakins back Sunday after Sunday. The pleasure was mutual. The two artists proved to be welcome guests. Eakins had found a new group of professional men with interesting minds. There was one difference; for the first time in his life, Eakins was in a relaxed social setting comprised solely of men, which he found both intriguing and comfortable. The only women, virtually invisible to visitors, were the nuns who cooked and cleaned for the seminarians.

Back in 1877, Eakins has been commissioned to paint James Frederick Wood, archbishop of Philadelphia. It is difficult now to imagine how real was the invisible barrier that existed between Protestant America and the growing number of the city's Catholics. As a young man, Eakins was a perfunctory anti-Catholic—before he met one. He came to admire Wood; the two became friendly, and Eakins produced a fine piece of work. With the painting completed, Eakins' tie to the Catholic world lapsed. No further church commissions came along; Eakins never painted a Protestant clergyman.

Now, a quarter of a century later, Eakins was not only enjoying the priests' company in their own home, he started painting them. He was at it from 1900 to 1903. He went to Cincinnati to paint the aged Archbishop William Henry Elder, to Washington for the portrait of Sebastiano Cardinal Martinelli. Other than his many pictures of musicians—cellists, oboists, singers, pianists, violinists—Eakins painted more of these Catholic clergymen than members of any other profession. One prelate, Patrick J. Garvey, on seeing the "ferocious" depiction of his face when shown the finished painting, is said to have hidden the canvas under his bed; others said it caught the monsignor's "irascible ways."[7] In perhaps the finest of the series, James P. Turner, of whom Eakins was particularly fond, holds his hand to his head and looks with calm, keen attention at his friend the artist.

In *The Translator*, Hugh Thomas Henry looks up from a Latin text. The portrait is one of the many that shows Eakins' thinkers and teachers sharing the canvas with the tools of their profession. (In no picture is this more prominent than in the huge painting of Sarah Sagehorn Frishmuth surrounded with her vast collection of musical instruments.)

Both the painter and the sculptor always had their eyes out for an interesting face or body. Some of Eakins' new friends proved compelling subjects. While Eakins was at his easel, Murray was molding clay for bronze castings. Today, St. Charles has six of Eakins' pictures of priests; Wood is there now as are Garvey, Turner, Loughlin, Henry, and one of a layman, a Knight of Columbus. Murray created a striking, beautifully executed life-sized bronze bust of a priest that remains in the seminary's collection. The rest of the twelve Eakins portraits of Catholic clergy ended up in other Catholic institutions across the country. Sylvan Schendler pointed out at forty years of age that a remarkable body of Eakins' work has never been given its due, largely because these portraits hang in the hallways or even back corners of Catholic rectories and hospitals rather than in public museums.[8] No exhibit has ever brought all or most of these pictures together.

Nothing could better illustrate the range of emotional terrain that Eakins traversed than these respites in Overbrook. The deep dips and sharp rises of his mental geography were pronounced; riding his bicycle out to spend quiet hours at the seminary provided a measure of the balance that the Avondale farm had for so long done. Balance, but more. St. Charles, though just outside the borders of Philadelphia, gave Eakins rich moments of repose.

The Thinker (Portrait of Louis N. Kenton), 1900.
(Metropolitan Museum of Art, New York)
See color plate 15.

XIX

A PAINTER AT WORK

EAKINS' INTERLUDE AT the seminary, during which, as always, he was painting, came in the midst of twenty years—bridging the nineteenth and twentieth centuries—in which he did his finest work. There would be no more lighthearted outdoors pictures, just serious portraits, largely of those whom Kathleen Foster has called Philadelphia's "teachers and thinkers," men from the professions and, in a very different light, women who lived on the edge of that world. Had he not been in Baltimore, Henry Rowland would have been the classic example of the former—a scientist, his helper, and the instruments of his field of knowledge.[1]

Back in 1889, fourteen years after Samuel Gross, another surgeon caught Eakins' eye. *The Agnew Clinic* of that year has a surgeon at work before a mass of students, much the same subject matter of *The Gross Clinic*. And yet, very different. Now Dr. D. Hayes Agnew stands in aristocratic profile while his surgical team performs a mastectomy. The first thing you notice, in sharp contrast to Dr. Gross's operating theater, is the predominance of white—Agnew's coat, the accompanying surgeons' jackets, and the nurse, white-caped. Medical history is on display. The germ theory had been learned in the interim between the paintings— all must now be as clean as the white pigment insists. The only thing not yet in use are the gloves to help ward off infection. Here Agnew brandishes a gleaming clean scalpel; gone is the scarlet gore of Dr. Gross's knife.

The students of the University of Pennsylvania's medical school commissioned the vast work, which, like its predecessor, was hung in their hospital and not in an art gallery. But while on display at the Academy of the Fine Arts, before finding its home, the painting was praised as *The Gross Clinic* had not been. Once more the anatomy of the patient is observed with great care. Eakins was in fact so profi-cient, so certain that anatomy was essential for painters that he lec-tured on the subject at the National Academy of Design in New York, and in classes in Brooklyn and Washington. By 1887, Eakins was on the board of the Art Students' League of New York, along with William Merritt Chase, Augustus Saint-Gaudens, and John H. Twachtman. He regularly taught not only anatomy, but classes in painting, first in their building on 23rd Street and later in their proud new quarters on 57th Street.[2]

In 1895, Eakins was asked to give his anatomy lectures at the Drexel Institute in Philadelphia. It is hard to believe, given the turmoil in 1887 at the academy, that once again he insisted on removing the loincloth from a male model and once again he was summarily fired. But Eakins was still trying to make a point, one that mattered greatly to him; as Walt Whitman had said, if the human body is not sacred, nothing is sacred.[3] There were letters to editors pointing out the silliness of the Drexel administration toward him, but the pungency that the issue still held is revealed in one personal letter Tom received: "I congratulate you on your success in raising a stir in prosaic Old Philadelphia. You have the warm approval & heart felt sympathy of all us Whitman fellows." But even this forthright approval of Eakins' action is coupled with the writer's misgivings: "I hold it to my own impurity that I cannot read

William Rush and His Model, 1908. (Honolulu Academy of Arts)

some Whitman's poems in any society."[4] Eakins, once again, had refused to concede that nakedness defied purity.

His teaching days over, Eakins took refuge in his studio with friends he wanted to paint. With one exception, he never again painted anyone nude; indeed all of his subjects were meticulously dressed. There is one strange picture of a female model frontally nude; she is a young lady of almost unreal pulchritude. You sense, as with *The Cruxifixion*, that Eakins felt compelled to paint a cliché of the art world, the luscious female nude. *William Rush and His Model* is a sort of Philadelphia Renoir, naked, but not sexy, a different breed from the women of his many psychologically deep portraits.

When Eakins turned to painting men of affairs, they appeared alone, often on large canvases. A perfect representative of these works is *Portrait of Leslie W. Miller*. Eakins' friend stands in the center of the picture holding a document and looking out as a confident male should. The painter

Portrait of Leslie W. Miller, 1901.
(Philadelphia Museum of Art)

Robert Henri admired the work: "This is what I call a beautiful portrait; not a pretty or swagger portrait, but an honest, respectful appreciative man-to-man portrait."[5]

Eakins gave the men he painted firmly planted feet; they look straight at you, masters of their world. If, out in that world, Eakins did not share the confidence that he perceived in these men, he was surely a master at the canvas. He perfectly captured a masterful cellist, Rudolph Hennig, in *The Cello Player*. The painter Ben Shahn, looking at this picture decades later found it "full of content, full of story, of perfection of likeness, of naturalness, of observation of small things—the look of wood and clothe [sic] and a face . . . [Eakins was] seeking to reveal character in his paintings"[6]

Louis Kenton provided a splendid exception. Eakins' 1900 painting of him displays neither the stolidity of his other male subjects, nor has he a face suffused with sadness. Instead, it is the picture of a man standing alone in an empty space, looking down. His feet are firmly on the ground, but his hands are helplessly crammed in his pockets. Kenton does not look out at the world, but stares at the floor. Perhaps the man's weakness was what Eakins wanted to explore. Just a year before, the forty-year-old Kenton married Elizabeth Macdowell, Eakins' sister-in-law. The couple moved into the Macdowell house, near the Eakinses' and lived there for two years before moving to their own place. All was not serene. Lid, as Susan called her sister, confided that Kenton had been violent toward her. Very soon after the move, the Macdowell family convened with Elizabeth and Louis present, and presumably admonished the husband and urged the wife to be "patient." A few weeks later Louis struck his wife in the face and, at midnight, she fled to Mt. Vernon Street—and stayed. Kenton left town. When Susan had to identify Kenton later, it was simply as "a friend of Mr. Eakins."[7]

Friend or foe, Eakins had found Kenton interesting enough to paint the year after he was married. Kenton was not a man of accomplishment. His marriage to Susan's sister was to be a disaster; the money they had had for their wedding trip to Europe was gone; he was a clerk. The picture of this lonely man was dubbed *The Thinker* when it was exhibited, in an attempt to explain his posture and gaze as contemplation rather than despair.

Another, very different portrait began with a preparatory sketch of the aristocratic Hayes Agnew that had been a study for *The Agnew Clinic*. Here, alone, he stands in elegant profile. A prospective buyer came to Eakins' studio and offered the painter $100 for it. Before completing the transaction, he brought a visiting German artist to see what he was purchasing. The German collector took one look and broke into a guffaw and said to Eakins, "Is he paying you a hundred dollars for that?"[8] Eakins did not have to court disaster—it came uninvited. Rather than reveling

Study for the Agnew Clinic, 1889.
(Yale University Art Gallery)

in the good reception of *The Agnew Clinic* itself, he smarted under the insult and leaned this portrait face to the wall behind a radiator in 1729 Mt. Vernon Street, as he had *Swimming* years before.

The young Philadelphia artist Robert Henri, beginning an energetic career, was a great admirer of Eakins. Henri was also coaching one of America's most eccentric and discerning collectors. Dr. Albert Barnes, rich from having developed Argyrol, a grim dark concoction that was crammed into the noses of reluctant children to thwart infection, was building a collection of impressionist paintings beyond comparison in America.

Samuel Murray, digging the Agnew portrait out from behind the radiator, urged Eakins to sell it. When it was put up for sale at the academy, Henri suggested to Barnes that he buy it. Barnes offered $3500 for it, Eakins insisted on more, and Barnes bought it for $4000, which, less the academy's commission, came to $3400, by far the largest sum Eakins ever received for a painting. The sale—or, even more, the negotiations over the painting—puts to rest any notion that Thomas Eakins was above the fray of commerce.

Congratulating Barnes on his purchase and frustrated in his efforts to champion Eakins' other work, Henri said, "I was cursing the luck that no big museum was forth coming with the sense or courage to buy Eakins' great masterpiece [*The Agnew Clinic*] and very much tempted to get into print about it, hopeless as the case might be."[9]

Many critics of Eakins' work speak of its dreary Victorian brown and fail to see how subtly he used the darkness to bring forth the richness of color. *The Concert Singer*, for example, has Weda Cook standing and singing—you can almost hear the song—in vivid silver-pink silk. Henri admired Eakins' sparing but telling uses of red—a color he himself put to good use. There is the red parasol of the passenger in *A May Morning in the Park*, the stocking and the toy truck of *Baby at Play*, and, notoriously, the scarlet of the blood on Dr. Gross's scalpel. One striking picture of an actress, Suzanne Santje, shows her elongated reclining body clothed in a striking red dress that trails to pink in a swirl of folds.

An Actress (Portrait of Suzanne Santje), 1903.
(Philadelphia Museum of Art)

As you come into a side room of the house that is the Phillips
Collection in Washington, D.C., and turn around, you are inches away
from *Portrait of Amelia C. Van Buren.* Squeezed into an ill-fitting out-
of-date pink dress, her elbow on an arm of the chair, her head resting
on her upraised hand, she looks away; is there deep meditation before
us, or is she simply sick and tired of posing? Van Buren had been a student of Eakins', was a longtime friend, and frequently modeled for his
camera. I find this one of Eakins' most fascinating and conflicted
paintings.

Portrait of Amelia C. Van Buren, c. 1891.
(The Phillips Collection, Washington, D.C.)
See color plate 16.

Portrait of Susan Macdowell Eakins (Mrs. Thomas Eakins), 1899.
(Hirshhorn Museum and Sculpture Garden)

Susan Macdowell Eakins, *Portrait of Thomas Eakins*, 1889.
(Philadelphia Museum of Art)

It is in the many portraits of women that Eakins' sensitivity is perhaps most on display. One after another, he shows women as introspective while the paintings of men depict confidences. Never is this more in evidence than in the greatest of many pictures of Sue that he painted at the end of the century. Her haunting face is alone in the upper left

Susan Macdowell Eakins. Photograph by Carl Van Vechten, 1938.
(Library of Congress)

quadrant of a relentlessly dark canvas. The handsome honesty of the picture is Eakins' finest tribute to his wife. It is striking how similar this
likeness of Sue at fifty is to the remarkable photograph Carl Van Vechten
took of her when she was in her eighties.

In 1892, Eakins' good friend Harrison Morris became the first professional director of the Academy of the Fine Arts, and Eakins' work, including a fine full-length profile portrait of Morris, was now hung
prominently in its shows. He, or at least his work, was back in the building in which his career had begun. But when Morris invited Eakins to
return to teach, he responded, "My honors are misunderstanding,
persecution and neglect, enhanced because unsought."[10] A splendid bit of
self-deprecation. Is it the whining of a hopeless misanthrope, filled with self-
pity, or a signal from a person who is suffering from deep depression?

Eakins wasn't as neglected an artist as his testy comments to Morris
would suggest. The Earles Galleries in Philadelphia gave him his only
solo show in 1896 and he had had works in the World's Columbian
Exposition in Chicago in 1893. He never saw his work in a solo show
in a major museum; it was just his luck that he died the year before the
Metropolitan Museum in New York mounted a splendid retrospective.

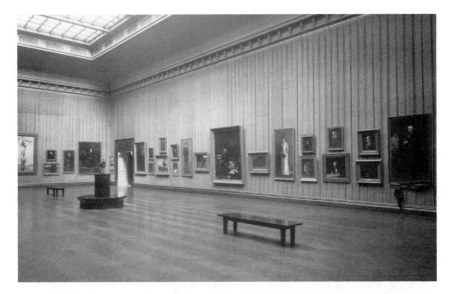

The Eakins Memorial Exhibition at the Metropolitan Museum of Art, New York, 1917. (Metropolitan Museum of Art, New York)

He must have known this was pending; such shows are not put together in ten minutes. Canvases must have been crated right under his nose, and it is sad that he never got to see an exhibit that was beautifully hung. The curator had a sixth sense of what mattered in Eakins' work. Centered on the main wall was *Swimming* with *The Gross Clinic* on its right and *The Thinker (Portrait of Louis W. Kenton)* on its left. Eakins' work was dismissed as old hat through much of the twentieth century; it was light-years away from the experiments of modernism. In 1933, Lloyd Goodrich published a two-volume work to restore Eakins to prominence. Half a century later, the rest of America woke up with the large Eakins show in Boston's Museum of Fine Arts, followed by the vast Philadelphia retrospective in 2001 that moved to the Metropolitan in New York. When it traveled to the Musée d'Orsay in Paris, Europe finally sat up and took notice.

The late paintings, as splendidly worked as they were, did not accomplish philosophically what Eakins had once aspired to. He had taken up the torch from optimists eager to pave the way to a new birth of freedom. His paintings would bring to bright reality the best America had to offer. They remain a great offering for us to celebrate; the wonderful

Self-Portrait, 1902. (National Academy Museum, New York)

windswept sailing on the Delaware or the charming look at a child at play were part of a world that went sour with the bitter ending of his career at the academy and the breach with his family when Ella killed herself. Eakins spent his last years painting the people at the end of the nineteenth century who could no longer embrace an idealistic world.

It was not, in the end, simply that the nineteenth century had let

Eakins down, but that it had let America down. Eakins himself had not failed, as his self-scorn would have it. It was his nineteenth century that, at its close, failed him. It had once promised fresh freedom, but as Eakins entered the twentieth century, his kind of painting would ring hollow. However Eakins' work is judged—not a few say it is America's finest—it could have been done only in the nineteenth century. The painter, any more than Thoreau or Douglass or Melville, could not get people to see the better world he had once depicted.

As America turned the corner into the twentieth century, Eakins was no more political than he had ever been. He died two years into a war that scarred the twentieth century and set the world on its troubled course. As survivors of that terrible century, experiencing the grim start of the twenty-first, we find kinship in Eakins' sense of the tragic quality of life.

Nowhere is this more apparent than in his self-portrait. As Philip Hamburger so aptly put it: "I have always found it a heartbreaking picture, as brutally honest as Rembrandt looking at Rembrandt. Eakins is left with few illusions. He sees himself straight. One feels that *he* feels that he has failed, but failed with indefatigable defiance."[11]

The painter had a message for his world, but the messenger never recovered from the terrible rebukes of his dismissal from the academy in 1886 or the banning from the Avondale farm in 1897. Eakins had escaped first to the Dakota Territory and then to Maine, but not for long. Each time, he had to come back to Philadelphia and to his regrets.

Defiantly, even as he failed, Eakins could not stop trying to make Philadelphia—America—become what he so badly wanted it to be. Worse, Eakins himself could not be what he knew he should be. His sexuality muffled, he had not been able to free himself to be the man he wanted to be, the naked man of *Swimming*. In nothing is his despair more evident than in this great self-portrait. He refused, as he had with other sitters, to disguise the face before him. Where once he swam naked into the sunlight, he was now stuffed into an ill-fitting suit, his face aching with disappointment. And, yet, here too defiant.

Mrs. Edith Mahon, 1904. (Smith College Museum of Art)
See color plate 1.

XX

Mrs. Edith Mahon

E VERY ATHLETE SHOULD be allowed to die looking like the sculpture *The Dying Gaul*, fit and powerful, tragically cut down in his prime. Thomas Eakins was not so lucky. At seventy-one, "he sort of went to pieces."[1] More accurately, he had been in declining health for six years. For the old athlete, still on his bicycle in his sixties, there has not been an accounting for this long debilitation. One speculation is that he was victim of the slow ravaging of lead poisoning. He used pigments every day of his life and was particularly fond of the white, so heavy with lead, which he used to prepare his canvases; this could have accounted for the gradual decline.[2] At the time, some thought he had been poisoned by milk, laced with formaldehyde added as a preservative. (He did drink huge amounts of milk, which was often treated with the chemical.) First corpulent, by 1916 he was frail and going blind.[3]

In Eakins' last year, Murray came to 1729 Mt. Vernon Street nearly every day to carry him piggyback down the stairs and help him onto the couch in the living room. One day, Sam saw Tom turn in the wrong

Eakins in His Mount Vernon Street Studio, c. 1909. Photographer unknown.
(Bryn Mawr College, Canaday Library, Seymour Adelman Collection)

direction when setting out for the dining room and realized the older man's eyesight was nearly gone. Talking after dinner about their jaunts on their bicycles and other exploits, Murray would get him back upstairs. Eakins found it hard to let him leave at the end of the evening. Desperately hanging on to his old friend, to life, he would, with trying pathos, tell Murray to be sure to come back the next day—"I'm kind of lonesome."[4]

Some of Eakins' old friends came to see him. When Harry Moore, his companion on the trips in Spain, arrived back in the United States to escape the ravages of the Great War he gave Eakins a great bear hug. Eakins' sign language came back to them as they reminisced. In 1916, Billy Smith came as well. By June Eakins could no longer get out of bed. He was, at the end, nursed by the three people who loved him most: Sue, Addie Williams, and Sam Murray, who recalled sitting at Tom's bedside holding his hand until he fell asleep. Sue would sit at the bedside through the night; on Sunday, June 25, Sam arrived and sent Sue down for some breakfast. When Tom woke up, Sam, trying to make conversation suddenly noticed that Eakins was no longer listening and his breathing was labored. He died that afternoon.

Tom's old student Tom Eagan, Harry Moore, and Sam Murray were pallbearers, as were Frederick Milligan, a physician who can be seen whispering to Eakins in the audience of *The Gross Clinic*; Gilbert Sunderland Parker, the curator of the Academy of the Fine Arts (which was still reluctant to allow him to mount an Eakins show); and Louis Husson, whose portrait Eakins had painted. Eakins was cremated; there was no service. Sue took the ashes back to 1729 Mt. Vernon Street; they were still there, on a shelf, when she died twenty-two years later. Murray took the ashes of them both to Woodlands Cemetery and buried them: "the last for the dearest friend I ever [k]new."[5]

Sue's true expression of her grief is on canvas, her *Thomas Eakins*. It is a marvelous painting, big and dark. The large canvas is both stronger than any of her other work and totally lacking in the femininity of the paintings of other women of her era, such as those of Mary Cassatt and Berthe Morisot. Kathleen Foster, who knows Eakins' work as no one else does, has said of the work, "Sue's portrait of Tom is much more intense than most of her work, and better (also bigger) than a lot of it . . . she was a very talented painter. But I think she worked on this over a long time as kind of grieving and for surrogate companionship, not to mention homage which I think explains its pitch. Knowing his wonderful portrait of her at the Hirshhorn, I have always thought of this as her memory of posing for him, a kind of through-the-looking glass turn about where the sitter becomes the painter."[6] Actually, he had sat for her; she had at least begun the picture in 1899, which does not detract from Foster's assessment.

Robert Henri, another painter touched by Eakins, paid his tribute in words: "His vision was not touched by fashion. He cared nothing for prettiness or cleverness in life or in art. He struggled to apprehend the constructive force in nature. . . . His quality was honest. 'Integrity' is the word which best suits him."[7]

Three-quarters of a century before Eakins painted his last great pictures, Beethoven composed his final pieces of music. There is a disjunc-
ture in comparing a composer's work to a painter's, but at least one of
Beethoven's late quartets, the composer's most poignant composition,
comes to mind. "That Opus 131 is a tragic work hardly needs further
explication," concludes Beethoven's recent biographer.[8] To some, the
subjective assigning of emotional value to music and paintings needs a
great deal of explicating, but, schooled as many of us are in western culture, it does not seem a stretch to detect a similarity of emotion in
Beethoven's music and in Eakins' painting. As the brilliant working of
the music reaches us, we hear tragedy. It was in the face of a pianist that
Eakins saw it most strongly. In that painting, we see it. Eakins saw in
Edith Mahon the weight of sorrow and conveys it in *Mrs. Edith Mahon*.

An artist who was almost exasperatingly scrupulous about the mathematical accuracy of his paintings was the master of conveying the personality of his sitters. Edith Mahon, looking at Eakins' statement of her,
might have said, like Velázquez's pope, "too real," too true. And she
would have been right; reality had been stretched to an almost unbear-
able point. With Edith Mahon, more powerfully than ever before,
Thomas Eakins saw another person's terrible defiant sadness reflecting
his own.

Sailboats Racing on the Delaware, 1874. (Philadelphia Museum of Art)

EPILOGUE

THE PHILADELPHIA MUSEUM of Art opened its temple atop a hill overlooking the Schuylkill River in 1928. Its energetic director, Fiske Kimball, was determined to give Philadelphia, belatedly, a collection worthy of the city. As he set out to build it, he asked William Ivins of the Metropolitan Museum in New York for tips and got a good one: "Go see the widow Eakins."[1] Within a year, Kimball had acquired the largest donation of a single artist's work that any American museum was to receive for three decades: eighty works in all, some of them among Eakins' finest work in oil, as well as drawings, bronzes, and wax figures.[2] And the gift came not solely from Susan Eakins, who, as executor of Tom's will, had sole responsibility for the disposal of the paintings. After the gift was made, plaques at the foot of the frame of one superb painting after another read: "Gift of Mrs. Thomas Eakins and Miss Mary Adeline Williams."

The impecunious spinster who, for three decades had depended on the kindness of kin, became one of the greatest donors to Mr. Kimball's museum, outshining any of Philadelphia's grandees. And the gift marked as well the friendship of the two women who made it. Addie was a second cousin of Will Crowell, Tom's estranged brother-in-law, so she and

Sigurd Fischer, *View of the Pennsylvania (Philadelphia)*
Museum of Art and the Fairmount Waterworks, 1928.
(Philadelphia Museum of Art)

Sue were related very remotely by marriage.[3] In his last will, signed in
1915, Eakins left one-quarter of the income from the trust that he had
established to Addie and three-quarters to Sue, but Sue was to be the sole
executor of the trust comprising a great many unsold paintings.[4] Sue was
not a professional widow, as she is sometimes made out to be. Rather, she
was a shrewd manager of the sale of some of Thomas Eakins' work and
gifts of the rest. It was a job that took faith and patience and cagey good
sense. The offer from the museum to take a large block of her husband's
paintings was "exactly the offer I wanted," she reported to Sam Murray.
"I want you particularly to know about it. Addie and I think it the finest
opportunity, and glad we can keep the pictures in Philadelphia."[5]

The Philadelphia Museum of Art became Thomas Eakins' home. Today, in a room devoted entirely to his work there hang some of his best-known paintings, some of the strongest work ever done by an American: *Shad Fishing at Gloucester, Sailboats Racing on the Delaware, Professionals at Rehearsal*. There is one exception: as you enter, you see Susan Eakins' arresting portrait of her husband. She sees, as do we, not only his unavoidable sadness, but, in his work, the transcendent beauty of an America gone by.

Tom was gone, but Sue's life went on. W. Douglass Paschall, the curator of the 2001 show of Susan Macdowell Eakins' work at the Woodmere Art Museum in Philadelphia, and long steeped in Eakins lore, speaks of the indisputably close relationship that existed between Susan and Addie, one that "wholly overwhelmed any connection that either had with Elizabeth," Sue's sister who shared the house with them after the collapse of her marriage.[6] Any remnant of pathetic spinsterhood that remained was gone. Addie shared her life with Sue for over twenty-two years.

Lucy Wilson, a staunch feminist friend of Susan, said that after Tom's death Sue "seemed to bloom all over again—started painting again."[7] Her greatest painting was of Thomas, a work that derives strongly from his portrait style. Only after Tom was dead and her tribute to her husband complete did Sue learn the lesson he had learned in Madrid: don't paint as your teacher painted, but as you alone see the world. In 1925, she painted a first-rate picture of a woman tennis player, racket held well, sneakered feet firmly on the court, ready for a game.[8] The fresh open picture is reminiscent of Tom's early sport pictures, though with a gentleness, even romanticism, that is Sue's alone.

She did not, to our knowledge, paint Addie, as Tom had twice done; Sue's canvases were few and far between.[9] Nor is there any photograph of Addie to equal Carl Van Vechten's superb study of Sue in the last year of her life. The dignity and elegance that had always been hers is only heightened in that handsome picture.

The house so long commanded by two larger-than-life men, was, after Tom died, a household of women. They lived on there for two

Professionals at Rehearsal, 1883. (Philadelphia Museum of Art)

decades. There was the Irish maid, assumed in most middle-class
American families, but seldom taken into account. Tuffy was the only
one of her names anyone seems to have remembered.[10] In addition,
Susan's sister, Elizabeth Macdowell Kenton, always a troubling presence,
made 1729 her home base in 1910. Lid (or Lizzie) was unlike her sister

Susan Macdowell Eakins, *The Tennis Player*, 1933.
(Bryn Mawr College, Canaday Library)

Sue in every way—certainly so in appearance: she was buxom while Sue
was gaunt. She projected a flirtatious manner as Sue never even thought
to do. Fortunately Elizabeth Kenton traveled a good deal. She lived for
a considerable time in a hotel in Manhattan (where she was known to
cabdrivers as "that crazy woman," since she simply held up her hands to

stop traffic and march straight out into it.)[11] Elizabeth was still making Mt. Vernon Street her home when Susan died in 1938 and the house had to be sold. She moved in with her brother in Roanoke, Virginia, surviving a quarter century until her death at the age of ninety-five.

And, of course, Addie. Mary Adeline Williams lived only another year or two after Susan Eakins died and a niece took her off to Washington, D.C. What was the nature of Sue and Addie's relationship? The joint gift to the Philadelphia Museum of Art makes it clear how central Sue thought it to be. There is no evidence, of course, of its being a sexual one, but, living hostage to the Great Man's unsold canvases, stacked against the walls of the house, we can perhaps hope that they found a chance at love out of the way of his shadow.

Thomas Eakins would have wanted them to.

NOTES ON SOURCES

THE MOST IMPORTANT source for a book about Thomas Eakins is not on paper, but on the walls of our museums. Fortunately, a large number of his paintings and photographs were gathered in the major retrospective of 2001, *Thomas Eakins: American Realist*, of which Darrel Sewell was the curator.

The immense catalogue for that show was a principal source for me: Darrell Sewell, ed., *Thomas Eakins* (Philadelphia: Philadelphia Museum of Art, 2001), abbreviated in the notes that follow as **Sewell, *Eakins Catalogue***. In addition to images of Eakins' work there are several long informative essays. There was not a day working on this book when I did not consult the catalogue; its thoroughness is marred only by the lack of an index.

Second only to the Sewell Catalogue is the invaluable Lloyd Goodrich, *Thomas Eakins*, 2 vols. (Cambridge: Harvard University Press, 1982), abbreviated in the notes as **Goodrich, *Thomas Eakins.*** Goodrich was the director of the Whitney Museum of American Art in New York City and a champion of Eakins. His earlier *Thomas Eakins:*

His Life and Work, published in 1933, is the basis for the two-volume work. Working when he did, Goodrich had the opportunity of interviewing many of Eakins' associates—most notably his widow, Susan Macdowell Eakins.

There is no "Thomas Eakins Papers" in the usual archival sense. The letters and other material by or about Thomas Eakins were read in three different forms. Those interested are referred to each site:

- Preparing for the 2001 Eakins retrospective, the Philadelphia Museum of Art amassed copies of much essential correspondence. This material is in the office of the curator of American art at the museum.

- The Pennsylvania Academy of the Fine Arts (PAFA), Eakins' home as a student and as a teacher (until his banishment), holds copies of many letters, which I read there. In 1984 the academy acquired the papers of Charles Bregler. Bregler was a student and friend of Eakins; on Susan Eakins' death, he acquired a large number of letters and photographs from the Eakins house. Some of the most critical letters by and about Eakins have been expertly transcribed in Kathleen A. Foster and Cheryl Leibold, *Writing About Eakins: The Manuscripts in Charles Bregler's Thomas Eakins Collection* (Philadelphia: University of Pennsylvania Press, 1989), abbreviated in the notes as **Foster and Leibold, *Writing.*** The book is also an invaluable general guide for research on Eakins, and it includes a cataloging of the entire Bregler Papers in PAFA on microfiche.

- In order to read all the letters in the Bregler Papers, I borrowed a set of microfiche from Amherst College and had them copied onto paper. Consisting of twelve bound volumes, these copies are now in the Special Collections of the Frost Library, Amherst College, Amherst, Massachusetts. The abbreviation **microfiche** in the notes refers to the full set of Bregler Papers, now available at Amherst in these two different forms.

NOTES

Dedication

Philip Hamburger, "Notes and Comment: Eakins in Boston," *The New Yorker*, October 25, 1982.

Preface: "It's Too Real"

1. I am indebted to Robert Campbell for this insight into Innocent's character.
2. On the excellent audio tour of the Palazzo Pamphilij, the English-speaking member of the family translates *e troppe vero* as "it's too real," in the sense of "too true."

Introduction

1. Henry David Thoreau, *Walden and other Writings of Henry David Thoreau* (New York: Modern Library, 1950), 7.

1. An Artist's Father

1. TE to Caroline Cowperthwait Eakins, October 1, 1866.
2. Richard Lewontin, *Ain't Necessarily So: The Dream of the Human Genome and Other Illusions* (New York: New York Review of Books, 2001), 193.

3. Ted A. Grossbart to the author, June 5, 2005.

4. Elizabeth LaMotte Cates Milroy, *Thomas Eakins' Artistic Training*, 1860–1870, (Ann Arbor, Mich.: University Microfilms, 1986), 73, n59; 74, n60.

5. The Dun Papers in the Baker Library, Harvard Business School, reveal no requests for credit by Benjamin Eakins or by any Cowperthwait. Any investments made by Benjamin Eakins would appear to have been made without borrowing. On the risks of investors using credit, see Scott Sandage, *Born Losers: A History of Failure in America* (Cambridge: Harvard University Press, 2005).

II. Central High School

1. *Handbook of the Central High School of Philadelphia* (Philadelphia: The Mary Gaston Barnwell Foundation, 1998), 153.

2. Ibid., 149.

3. Ibid.

4. Ibid., 150.

5. Ibid., 151.

6. David F. Labaree, *The Making of the American High School: The Credentials Market and the Central High School of Philadelphia* (New Haven: Yale University Press, 1988).

7. *Handbook of Central High School*, 154.

8. Goodrich, *Thomas Eakins*, 1:5.

9. TE to Benjamin Eakins, March 6, 1868, in Foster and Leibold, *Writing*, 207.

10. Labaree, *Making of American High School*, 24–25, 145–46.

11. The archives of Central High School; the catalogue of 1853 seems to have sufficed for years Eakins was in attendance.

12. Kathleen A. Foster, *Thomas Eakins Rediscovered* (New Haven: Yale University Press, 1997). The chapter "The Rowing Pictures: A Passion for Perspective" (123–30), is a tour de force of analysis and demonstrates how essential Eakins thought precision to be. See also Kathleen A. Foster, ed., *A Drawing Manual by Thomas Eakins* (Philadelphia: Philadelphia Museum of Art, 2005).

13. Program of Graduation Exercises, Sartain Papers, microfilm roll 4235, Archive of American Art, Smithsonian Institution, Washington, D.C.

14. Elizabeth Johns, quoted in Elizabeth LaMotte Cates Milroy, *Thomas Eakins' Artistic Training, 1860–1870* (Ann Arbor, Mich.: University Microfilms, 1986), 49.

III. Four Uneventful Years?

1. Michael Fried, *Realism, Writing, Disfiguration* (Chicago: University of Chicago Press, 1987), passim. Fried discusses Eakins use of calligraphy in his work as the "materiality" of words.

2. Gary B. Nash, *First City: Philadelphia and the Forging of Historical Memory* (Philadelphia: University of Pennsylvania Press, 2002), 141.

3. Earl Shinn, "A Philadelphia Art School," *The Art Amateur*, January 10, 1884, 32, quoted in Elizabeth LaMotte Cates Milroy, *Thomas Eakins' Artistic Training, 1860–1870* (Ann Arbor, Mich.: University Microfilms, 1986), 54–55.

4. Nash, *First City*, 193.

5. TE to Albert B. Frost, June 8, 1888.

6. William S. McFeely, *Frederick Douglass* (New York: Norton, 1991), 114.

7. Nash, *First City*, 168.

8. Ibid., 233.

9. Tucked away in a dissertation endnote, Elizabeth Milroy, who, I suspect, was an antiwar undergraduate in the 1960s, displays the skill of a P. D. James and unearths two clues that suggest that Eakins skipped town in 1865. In that year, he is not listed in the Philadelphia City Directory, as he had been in previous years; more ingenious still, she notes an Eakins letter from Europe that describes some English officers in Montreal—a city he is not known ever to have visited. Mid-nineteenth-century draft dodging required only the payment of a bounty fee, which Eakins had done in 1864, not trips to Canada. But this intriguing trivia underscores how elusive Eakins story is in this decade. Milroy, *Thomas Eakins' Artistic Training*, 75, n60.

10. TE to Caroline Cowperthwait Eakins, October 1, 1866.

11. Ibid.

12. Ibid.

13. Ibid.

IV. ÉCOLE DES BEAUX-ARTS

1. Georges-Eugène Haussmann was chosen by Louis Napoleon to undertake the vast urban renewal operation in Paris that cleared much of medieval Paris and opened the city's broad boulevards. See, e.g., Alistair Horrne, *Seven Ages of Paris* (New York: Knopf, 2002), 233–35.

2. TE to Caroline Cowperthwait Eakins, October 8, 1866.

3. Ibid.

4. TE to Benjamin Eakins, October 13, 1866, in Foster and Leibold, *Writing*, 193, 195.

5. TE to Benjamin Eakins, October 26–27, 1866, in ibid., 199.

6. Ibid., 200.

7. Ibid., 201.

8. Ibid., 201, 202.

9. TE to Benjamin Eakins, November 1, 1866, in ibid., 204, 205.

10. Ibid, 205.

11. TE to Benjamin Eakins, November 1867.

12. Earl Shinn to his parents, October 1866, Earl Shinn Papers and Diary, Smithsonian Institution Research System microfilm.

13. TE to Benjamin Eakins, November 1867.

14. Goodrich, *Thomas Eakins*, 1:21.

V. LUXEMBOURG GARDEN

1. H. Barbara Weinberg, "Studies in Paris and Spain," in Sewell, *Eakins* Catalogue, 13–26; quotations from 18, 19.

2. TE to Benjamin Eakins, quoted in ibid., 17.

3. TE to Benjamin Eakins, March 5, 1868, in Foster and Leibold, *Writing*, 206.

4. Graham Robb, *Strangers: Homosexual Love in the Nineteenth Century* (New York: Norton, 2004), 30.

5. Anna Klumpke, *Rosa Bonheur: The Artist's (Auto)biography*, trans. Gretchen van Slyke (Ann Arbor, Mich.: University of Michigan Press, 1997).

6. Ibid., photocopy of *prefect de police*'s authorizing Bonheur to "*s'habiller en homme*," May 12, 1857, and photograph of Bonheur reclining with lion's club, both following 197 (this book's

photo section also features a wonderfully loony photograph of Bonheur with Buffalo Bill Cody on his 1883 Parisian visit—apparently, American gunnery appealed to her). See also Dore Ashton and Denise Browne Hare, *Rose Bonheur* (New York: Viking, 1981), 70.

7. Ashton and Hare, *Rosa Bonheur*, 57, 59.

8. TE to Frances Eakins, February 1868.

9. William Sartain quoted in Goodrich, *Thomas Eakins*, 1:33.

10. Emily Sartain to TE, July 8, 1868.

11. Ibid.

12. Ibid.

13. Ibid.

14. TE to Emily Sartain, July 1868, Pennsylvania Academy of the Fine Arts.

15. Robb, *Strangers*, p. 12.

16. Emily Sartain, with Eakins' help, became head of the Moore School, an institution for women, and had a record as a progressive teacher. She never married.

VI. SPAIN

1. H. Barbara Weinberg, "Studies in Paris and Spain," in Sewell, *Eakins* Catalogue, 13–26; quotation from 19.

2. Goodrich, *Thomas Eakins*, 1:54.

3. Jean-Léon Gérôme's painting—with the Latin title *Ave Caesar, Morituri Te Salutant*—can be seen in the Yale University Art Gallery in New Haven. *The Nymph and Eros* is at the Clark Museum, Williamstown, Massachusetts.

4. TE, "Spanish Notebook" (notebook of the trip to Spain, in the archive of the Philadelphia Museum of Art).

5. Ibid.

6. Ibid., Rachel Brown and Daniel Dejean, e-mail to author, June 21, 2004. See also H. Barbara Weinberg, "Studies in Paris and Spain," in Sewell, *Eakins* Catalogue, 13–26, 23.

7. William Sartain diary, transcript in archive of the Philadelphia Museum of Art.

8. Quoted in Goodrich, *Thomas Eakins*, 1:55; Eakins knew English, his high school Latin and Greek, German, French, Italian, and now Spanish. He could also sign.

9. TE to Benjamin Eakins, January 16, 1870, quoted in ibid.

10. TE to Benjamin Eakins, March 29, 1870, quoted in ibid., 57.

11. TE to Benjamin Eakins, January 16, 1870, quoted in ibid., 55.

12. Sartain diary.

13. The "Spanish Notebook" could have been written on this trip to Madrid, but its tone suggests the excitement of a first visit to the Prado. The notes reflect a concentration not available with two friends along. A notebook would be in the way when using sign language.

VII. PHILADELPHIA

1. Gary B. Nash, *First City: Philadelphia and the Forging of Historical Memory* (Philadelphia: University of Pennsylvania Press, 2002), 152.

2. Actually, Eakins denied both men names. He distributed the painting with only its generic name, *Rail Shooting, on the Delaware*. See Kathleen A. Foster, *Eakins Rediscovered* (New Haven: Yale University Press, 1998), 138, 366–67, citing Martin Berger who identified the "black-man" as Dave Wright and asserts his primacy in the painting.

3. Charles Rosenberg, e-mail to author, July 19, 2004.

4. *Frank Leslie's Historical Register of the Centennial Exposition* (New York: Frank Leslie's Publishing House, 1877), 65 and *passim*.

5. Justin Kaplan, *Walt Whitman* (New York: Simon and Schuster, 1980), 351.

VIII. WORKSHOP

1. F. O. Matthiessen, *American Renaissance: Art and Expression in the Age of Emerson and Whitman* (New York: Oxford University Press, 1941), 606.

2. Maria Jo Chamberlin-Hellman, "Thomas Eakins as a Teacher" (Ph.D. diss., Columbia University, 1981), 127.

3. Ibid., 128.

4. The first level of instruction was known as the "antique (drawing from casts)"; the advanced course was "Life Drawing (drawing and painting from live models)". The men's class met every afternoon (except Sunday); the women's, three mornings a week. Rules outlining what would be the pose of the model were carefully laid out; a different group of five students would decide, on a rotating basis, what the pose should be. Pennsylvania Academy of the Fine Arts, "Circular: Committee of Instruction, 1879–80," on microfiche.

5. Thomas Eakins was guilty of having written a textbook. Recently reprinted (Kathleen A. Foster, ed., *A Drawing Manual by Thomas Eakins* [Philadelphia: Philadelphia Museum of Art, 2005]), it is a manual that gives undoubted evidence of Eakins' seriousness as an art teacher. It is clear from the extensive notes that one student, Charles Bregler, kept that Eakins was a painstaking teacher.

6. Chamberlin-Hellman, "Eakins as Teacher," 197.

7. Charles Bregler, notes on class at Art Students League, 1887.

8. Chamberlin-Hellman, "Eakins as Teacher," 194.

9. Horatio Shaw to Susan Shaw, September 5, 1880.

10. Ibid.

11. Horatio Shaw to Susan Shaw, December 19, 1880.

12. John Henry Hepp IV, *The Middle-Class City: Transforming Space and Time in Philadelphia, 1876–1926* (Philadelphia: University of Pennsylvania Press, 2003), 79; Horatio Shaw to Susan Shaw, November 17, 1880.

IX. PAINTER AND SCIENTIST

1. Gordon Hendricks, "The Eakins Portrait of Rutherford B. Hayes," *The American Art Journal*, Spring 1969, 104–14; quotation from 105.

2. Ibid., 105.

3. TE to Charles Henry Hunt, quoted in ibid., 112; TE to Kathrin Crowell, August 19, 1877.

4. James W. Crowell, "Recollections of Life on the Crowell Farm," ed. Betty Crowell, in *Eakins*, (Chadds Ford, Pa.: Brandywine River Museum, 1980), 15–17.

5. I am indebted to Martha Mahard for identifying his camera.

6. For a detailed description of how Eakins worked, based on infrared readings of his canvases, see Mark Tucker and Nica Gutman, "Photographs and the Making of Photographs," in Sewell, *Eakins* Catalogue, 225–36.

7. When Rafael Soyer, a mid-twentieth-century realist and admirer of Eakins, approvingly said, "I would think Eakins used photography to some extent in his paintings," Lloyd Goodrich, thinking Eakins should be defended against such an accusation, replied "No, he did not," Rafael Soyer, *Homage to Thomas Eakins, Etc.* (South Brunswick, N.J.: Thomas Yoseloff, 1966), 19.

8. University of Pennsylvania, *Animal Locomotion: The Muybridge Work at the University of Pennsylvania* (Philadelphia: University of Pennsylvania Press, 1888), 6 (Allen), 9 (Marks).

9. Horton A. Johnson and Caryl D. Johnson, "The Clinical Eye of Thomas Eakins," *The Pharos*, Summer 2005, 28–29; quotation from 28. (Thanks to Richard Kerber.)

10. Philip Hamburger, "Eakins in Boston," *The New Yorker*, October 25, 1982; Eliza McFeely, *Zuni and the American Imagination*. (New York: Hill and Wang, 2001), 114–15. Stewart Culin was a distinguished anthropologist and a good friend of Eakins. Eakins painted a large portrait of him, possibly a partner of the Cushing picture. Culin's widow told Lloyd Goodrich in 1930 that it had been stolen; perhaps she had destroyed it. Its recovery would be welcome.

X. SUE

1. Goodrich, *Thomas Eakins*, 2:81, and most subsequent studies.

2. TE to Kathrin Crowell, August 22, 1874; her letters to him are lost. William Crowell, Kathrin's brother, was married to Eakins' sister Frances.

3. Nancy Garrett, telephone conversation with author, July 21, 2004.

4. TE to Arthur B. Frost, June 8, 1887, a letter in which Eakins rebuts a rumor that he and Susan were not married: "there was nothing irregular in our marriage which was in the Quaker form and registered and published in the daily papers."

5. See, for example, Jeanette M. Toohey, "Susan Eakins: A Modest Reappraisal," in *Susan Eakins (1851–1938)*, exhibition catalogue, Woodmere Art Museum, Philadelphia, September 16–December 9, 2001.

6. These quotations are in the Bregler Papers at the Pennsylvania Academy of the Fine Arts.

7. Ibid. See Walt Whitman, *Complete Poetry and Collected Prose* (New York: Library of America, 1982): *Calamus*, "When I Heard at the Close of the Day," p. 276, and "Song of the Broad Axe," p. 339. The copier made slight inconsequential changes.

8. Susan Macdowell Eakins' collateral heirs are dismayed by the casual scattering of her work after her death.

XI. SCULPTURE AND PHOTOGRAPHY

1. Michael W. Panhorst, "The Equestrian Sculptures for the Brooklyn Memorial Arch," in *Eakins* (Chadds Ford, Pa.: Brandywine River Museum, 1980), 24–26.

2. J. Laurie Wallace in interview with Lloyd Goodrich, March 24, 1938.

3. Art critic Peter Schjeldahl regards *The Crucifixion* as Eakins' worst painting.

4. Susan Danly and Cheryl Leibold, eds., *Eakins and the Photograph: Works by Thomas Eakins and His Circle in the Collection of the Pennsylvania Academy of the Fine Arts* (Washington, D.C.: Smithsonian Institute Press, 1994), 69.

5. Many of Eakins' photographs were on display in the 2001 retrospective, but largely to throw light on his paintings. A show of his photographs alone would enable their artistic merit to be fully evaluated.

XII. SWIMMING

1. Thomas Anschutz to John Laurie Wallace, quoted in Goodrich, *Thomas Eakins*, 1:237; Stephen Greenblatt, *Will in the World: How Shakespeare Became Shakespeare* (New York: Norton, 2004), 233.

2. Marc Simpson, "Swimming Through Time: An Introduction," in Doreen Bogler and Sarah Cash, eds., *Thomas Eakins and the Swimming Picture* (Fort Worth: Amos Carter Museum, 1996), 1–12; quotation from 3. This is an intelligent, thoughtful essay.

3. Ibid., 3.

4. Sarah Cash, "Biographies of Models for *Swimming*," in ibid., 117–22; Benajmin Fox is the figure in the water with Eakins' setter, Harry; Talcott Williams is the reclining figure, J. Laurie Wallace the one sitting, Jesse Godley standing, and George Reynolds diving; if, as J. Laurie Wallace claimed and Charles Bregler confirmed, Wallace was a subject of the picture, Eakins or a colleague must have taken the photographs from which Eakins worked no later than 1882. Wallace was living in Chicago in 1885 when Eakins painted the picture (and Anschutz reported this fact to Wallace).

5. Philip Cafaro, *Thoreau's Living Ethics: Walden and the Pursuit of Virtue* (Athens: University of Georgia Press, 2004), 19.

6. Simpson, "Swimming Through Time," 10, n5, 4, 5, 6.

7. F. O. Matthiessen, *American Renaissance: Art and Expression in the Age of Emerson and Whitman* (New York: Oxford University Press, 1941), 610.

8. Oliver Larkin, *Art and Life in America* (New York: Holt Rinehart and Winston, 1960), 278.

9. Eakins himself could be unthinking about African Americans; he was not above referring, in passing, to "ragged old niggers."

10. Arthur Danto, "Men Bathing," *ART News*, March 1995, 95; Linda Nochlin quoted in Simpson, "Swimming Through Time," 6; Peter Schjeldahl, "Greek Gifts," *The New Yorker*, August 4, 2004, 66.

11. Thomas H. Johnson, ed., *The Complete Poems of Emily Dickinson* (Boston: Little Brown, 1960), #540. 263.

XIII. THE ACADEMY

1. Beulah M. Rhoades to Caleb Cope, January 15, 1885.

2. "R.S." to E. H. Coates, April 11, 1882.

3. E. H. Coates to TE, November 27, 1885.

4. E. H. Coates to J. W. Corliss, May 16, 1885.

5. Kathleen A. Foster, "Eakins and the Academy," in Sewell, Eakins Catalogue, 104.

6. Sylvan Schendler, *Thomas Eakins* (Boston: Little Brown, 1967), 94.

7. Students to the Board of Directors of the Academy, February 15, 1886.

8. Schendler, *Thomas Eakins*, 95.

9. John P. Kelly et al. to Board of Directors of Academy, March 12, 1886.

10. William Crowell to TE, April 26, 1886, in Foster and Leibold, *Writing*, 225.

11. TE to Fanny Eakins Crowell, June 4, 1886, in ibid., 226–27.

XIV. DAKOTA

1. TE to Fanny Eakins Crowell, June 4, 1886, in Foster and Liebold, *Writing*, 236.

2. Jeanette Marks Papers, Mount Holyoke Archives, South Hadley, Massachusetts; William Marks's daughter, Jeanette, born in 1875, was eleven when Eakins was at their summer house in Westport, New York.

3. S. Weir Mitchell, "Nervousness and Its Influence on Character," in *Medicine and Society in America* (1888; reprint, New York: Arno, 1972), 116.

4. Ibid., 120.

5. TE to Benjamin Eakins, October 26, 1866, in Foster and Leibold, *Writing*, 201.
6. Anna Robeson Burr, *Weir Mitchell: His Life and Letters* (New York: Duffield, 1929), 178.
7. TE to Susan Macdowell Eakins, July 13, 1887.
8. TE to Susan Macdowell Eakins, August 28, 1887, in Foster and Leibold, *Writing*, 240–42.
9. TE to Susan Macdowell Eakins, August 30, 1887, in ibid., 242–43.
10. Ibid.
11. TE to J. Laurie Wallace, December 8, 1887.
12. Ibid.

xv. Mickle Street

Horace Traubel's *With Walt Whitman in Camden* is an invaluable primary source for the Whitman-Eakins friendship. Over the past century, this memoir has been published in various forms, and each of the three editions I consulted includes material that the other two have omitted. To simplify citations in this chapter's notes, I use these abbreviations, based on each edition's publication date:

• The 4-volume set issued by Small, Maynard (Boston, 1906) is cited as Traubel 1906.
• The 4-volume set from the University of Pennsylvania Press (Philadelphia, 1953) is cited as Traubel 1953.
• In 1996, W. L. Bentley Rare Books in Oregon House, California, published two so-called closing volumes of Traubel's series, labeled Volume 8: *February 11–September 30, 1891*, and Volume 9: *October 1, 1891–April 3, 1892*. These are cited as Traubel 1996, with the corresponding volume number.

1. Traubel 1953, vol. 4, *January 21–April 17, 1889*, 155.
2. Ibid., 135.
3. Justin Kaplan, *Walt Whitman* (New York: Simon and Schuster, 1980), 367.
4. Traubel 1953, vol. 4, 155.
5. J. M. Coetzee, "Love and Walt Whitman," *New York Review of Books*, September 25, 2005, 22–57; quotation from 26.
6. Ibid., 26.
7. Ibid.
8. Traubel 1953, vol. 4, 155.
9. Traubel 1906, vol. 1, 367.
10. Traubel quoted in Goodrich, *Thomas Eakins*, 2:34.
11. Traubel *[which edition?]*, vol. 4, 104.
12. Traubel 1996, vol. 8, *February 11–September 30, 1891*, 202.
13. Traubel 1906, vol. 1, 41.
14. Ibid., 284.
15. Traubel 1996, vol. 8, 41.
16. Ibid., 603–4.
17. Weda Cook in conversation with Lloyd Goodrich, *Thomas Eakins*, 2:38.

xvi. Ella

1. Newspaper clipping from local press on inquest into Ella Crowell's death, dated July 5, 1897 by hand, Philadelphia Museum of Art.

2. RG 1050.002, Coroner's Office, Coroner's Docket 1897–1905, Chester County (Pa.) Archives and Records Services. (Thanks to Laurie Rofino.) The Commonwealth of Pennsylvania denied my request to see the Ella Crowell records from the Norristown State Hospital, as the Norristown Asylum for the Insane is now known.

3. Jules David Prown, "Thomas Eakins' *Baby at Play*," *Studies in the History of Art* 18 (1985), 121—27; quotation from 125.

4. Susan Macdowell Eakins, memorandum, 1897(?) in Foster and Liebold, *Writing*, 290–98; quotation from 296.

5. Goodrich, *Thomas Eakins*, 2:135.

6. Susan Macdowell Eakins to Fanny Eakins Crowell, October 18, 1896.

7. James W. Crowell, "Recollections of Life on the Crowell Farm," ed. Betty Crowell, in *Eakins* (Chadds Ford, Pa.: Brandywine River Museum, 1980), 15–17; quotation from 17.

8. It is sad to read a letter from Will Crowell to his old friend addressed to "Mr. T. C. Eakins." Crowell tells of a crop failure and threatened mortgage foreclosure and then asks if there was any residue of Eliza Cowperthwait's estate that her niece (his wife, Fanny) might obtain. No reply is known. William Crowell to TE, August 14, 1899.

XVII. MOUNT DESERT

1. Henry Adams, *The Education of Henry Adams* (1918; reprint, New York: Modern Library, 1996).

2. Richard Lewontin, e-mail to author, July 7, 2003.

3. TE to Susan Macdowell Eakins, n.d. [c. July 22, 1897].

4. Ibid.

5. Ibid.

6. TE to Susan Macdowell Eakins, n.d. [1897].

7. TE to Susan Macdowell Eakins, n.d. [c. August 1, 1897].

8. Goodrich, *Thomas Eakins*, 2:143.

9. Ibid.

10. Ibid.

11. TE to Susan Macdowell Eakins, August 11, 1897.

12. Ibid.

13. TE to Susan Macdowell Eakins, n.d. [c. August 6, 1897].

14. TE to Susan Macdowell Eakins, n.d. [c. July 31, 1897].

15. TE to Susan Macdowell Eakins, n.d. [c. August 1, 1897].

16. TE to Susan Macdowell Eakins, n.d. [c. early August 1897].

17. TE to Susan Macdowell Eakins, n.d.

18. TE to Susan Macdowell Eakins, n.d.

19. The Museum of Fine Arts, Boston, has no record of which Sargents were on display.

20. Goodrich, *Thomas Eakins*, 2:144.

XVIII. SAMUEL MURRAY

1. Margaret McHenry, *Thomas Eakins Who Painted* (privately printed, 1946), 133.

2. Susan Macdowell Eakins diary, June 4, 1899, on microfiche.

3. Goodrich, *Thomas Eakins*, 2:99.

4. Ibid., 101.

5. Ned Rorem quoted in Henry Adams, *Eakins Revealed: The Secret Life of an American Artist* (New York: Oxford University Press, 2005), 307.

6. Goodrich, *Thomas Eakins*, 2:144.

7. Ibid., 192.

8. Sylvan Schendler, *Thomas Eakins* (Boston: Little Brown, 1967), 211.

XIX. A PAINTER AT WORK

1. Kathleen A. Foster, "Portraits of Teachers and Thinkers," in Sewell, *Eakins* Catalogue, 307–15.

2. Holland Cotter, "A School's Colorful Patina," *The New York Times*, September 9, 2005. The league is credited with being the institution where modern art began in America, a departure to which Eakins can be tied by inspiration. Robert Henri, who greatly admired his older fellow Philadelphia painter, moved to New York and became a mainstay of the teaching faculty of the New York league. It has been said that "institutionally, modern art began with Henri."

3. Walt Whitman, *Leaves of Grass* (New York: Norton, 1973), 99.

4. A. R. Wilcraft to TE, March 15, 1895.

5. Robert Henri, *The Art Spirit* (Philadelphia: Lippincott, 1951), 91.

6. Ben Shahn, *The Shape of Content* (Cambridge: Harvard University Press, 1957), 72.

7. Foster, "Portraits of Teachers," 420, n20, citing Carol Troyen.

8. Goodrich, *Thomas Eakins*, 2:267.

9. Ibid. Henri seems to be wishing the painting was in a large public museum, rather than at the medical school.

10. Carol Troyen, "Eakins in the Twentieth Century," in Sewell, *Eakins* Catalogue, 367–76; quotation from 367.

11. Philip Hamburger, "Notes and Comment: Eakins in Boston," *The New Yorker*, October 25, 1982.

XX. MRS. EDITH MAHON

1. Goodrich, *Thomas Eakins*, 2:271.

2. If so, Eakins was in good company; Goya is said to have suffered from lead poisoning.

3. Goodrich, *Thomas Eakins*, 2:272.

4. I am indebted to Goodrich's account of Eakins death. He had discussed it with Samuel Murray.

5. Goodrich, *Thomas Eakins*, 2:272.

6. Kathleen Foster, e-mail to author, January 16, 2004.

7. Robert Henri, *The Art Spirit* (Philadelphia: Lippincott, 1951), 91.

8. Louis Lockwood, *The Music and the Life of Beethoven* (New York: Norton, 2003), 488.

EPILOGUE

1. Goodrich, *Thomas Eakins*, 2:282.

2. In 1968, an even larger group of Edward Hopper's work went to the Whitney Museum in New York.

3. Margaret McHenry, *Thomas Eakins Who Painted* (privately printed, 1946), 131.

4. Goodrich, *Thomas Eakins*, 2:273; Philadelphia *Bulletin*, September 5, 1940.

5. Susan Macdowell Eakins to Samuel Murray, November 30, 1929, quoted in Goodrich, *Thomas Eakins*, 2:282.

6. W. Douglass Paschall, e-mail to author, June 15, 2004.

7. Lucy Langston W. Wilson in interview with Lloyd Goodrich, May 21, 1930, Philadelphia Museum of Art.

8. Cover illustration, *Susan Eakins (1851–1938)*, exhibition catalogue, Woodmere Art Museum, Philadelphia, September 16–December 9, 2001.

9. Susan had no one to look after her work when she died as she meticulously had done with her husband's paintings when he died. There may have been sketches and canvases that have been lost.

10. Henry Adams, *Eakins Revealed: The Secret Life of an American Artist* (New York: Oxford University Press, 2005), 6.

11. Nancy Garrett to W. Douglass Paschall, July 12, 2004.

ACKNOWLEDGMENTS

A HOST OF PEOPLE helped me with this book. Many archivists and reference librarians, whose names I did not always get, answered queries by e-mail and telephone. I can only apologize if I fail to recall all of those who gave me assistance.

First, my thanks go to Kathleen A. Foster, curator of American art at the Philadelphia Museum of Art and, more importantly, an expert on Eakins. Rather than being dismayed at a historian invading art history territory, she welcomed me and offered indispensable help. Scarcely less so was the assistance I received from her assistant, Audrey Lewis. Darrel Sewell had retired before I went to work, but as the curator of the great *Thomas Eakins, American Realist* show of 2001 and editor of its catalogue, he was, in a sense, at my right hand daily.

Douglass Paschall was his assistant when that show was being put together, and he took me behind the scenes to view *Swimming*—the real thing—for the first time. Doug has encouraged me every step of the way; he deserves great credit for giving Susan Macdowell Eakins her due with a show of her work at the Woodmere Art Museum. Another art historian (and former colleague), Paul Staiti, provided a discriminating reading of the penultimate manuscript. Cheryl Leibold, archivist of the Pennsylvania Academy of the Fine Arts—which holds the essential Eakins material in its Bregler Collection—and herself an Eakins expert, was also helpful.

Navigating Philadelphia waters, I received assistance from a myriad of people. First Lucy and Sheldon Hackney provided bed and breakfast and great company when I was in town. More formally, a joint fellowship from the Library Company of Philadelphia and the Historical Society of Pennsylvania provided valuable help as I began this project. I am indebted to John C. Van Horne, director of the Library Company; David Molke-Hansen, president of the historical society; and members of their staffs, in particular Jim Green and Sarah J. Weatherwax at the Library Company. Research help also came from Christine Van Horne.

Assistance was given by Dr. Bernard A. Sanders, the archivist of the remarkable Central High School. One of its alumni, Mark Klugheit (whom I recalled well from his Yale days), attempted, with David Haendler, to obtain the medical records of Ella Crowell. When tracking the Crowell family, Laurie Rofino, Chester County's director of archives, and her sister, Diane Rofino, at the Chester County Historical Society were a big help. Though we never got to make the trip, I somehow knew the area by talking with my grade-school friend Dave Ryerson.

Across the Delaware River, Leo K. Blake showed me around the Walt Whitman house, and, not far from the Schuylkill River, Todd Wilmot took me on a tour of St. Charles Borromeo Seminary. Cait Kokolus, the seminary's librarian, also was a help. William J. Lanouette taught me a bit about Philadelphia's famous boat clubs, and Will Schmitt did his best to explain to me how to row a scull. Frank Wilson, book editor of the *Philadelphia Inquirer*, posted my request for information; Annie K. V. Klotz responded to the inquiry with useful newspaper clippings; Shanlee Pollack also responded.

I cannot fault the able librarians at the University of Pennsylvania; it is not their fault that Penn's distinguished scientists in Eakins' time did not leave more complete papers to document their achievements. Michael Ryan and his associates cheerfully helped with the holdings they have. Other archivists, notably Charles Greifenstein at the College of Physicians, hunted for material on the various physicians important to Eakins.

Farther afield, Eleanor Munro shared her enthusiasm for Eakins, and Peter Lax alerted me to Fairfield Porter's fondness for Eakins. In Paris, Vassela Kamazieva at the Musée d'Orsay led me to the only Eakins in a public museum in Paris. (I am still astonished by the paucity of his work in European art collections.) Joshua Cole was a good friend steering me through nineteenth-century French history. R. L. Wilson gave an assist on the unlikely subject of guns in nineteenth-century Paris. Michelle Trozier-Chenyne did some work guiding me through Paris archives. Hunter S. Frost reported in on Gérôme's visit to the United States, and Jane Dow Bromberg located Eakins' address in Paris for me. Charles Rosenberg informed me on medical matters. Robert Shilkret and Ted A. Grossbart checked my thinking on matters psychological. Paul Wright pointed out Eakins' profound influence on Leonard Baskin's work. Will Smethurst gave me his learned thoughts on Eakins and modernism.

I am extremely grateful to Professor Margery Garber and Mary Halpenny-Killip at the Harvard Humanities Center where I have had the good fortune of being an associate fellow. I can scarcely begin to thank satisfactorily the many people at the incomparable Harvard Libraries; I don't even know the names of many people in reference who answered inquiries and hunted down material. Always knowledgeable was Joe Borneuf at the Widener Library; in the Fine Arts Library, Martha R. Mahard came up with information on Eakins' camera, the Scoville; and Hunt Luker, Sarah Hambelton, and Matthew Preisma in the often-unheralded Interlibrary Loan Department were very resourceful.

In the post-typewriter world, computer tech support is as indispensable as patience, and the vast network of people offering this service at Harvard has been wonderfully helpful. In particular I want to thank

Shannon Brantley, James Kelley, Matthew Wollman, Anthony Quinn, and Jamesley Dasse.

Indispensable to a book about Eakins were, of course, pictures of his work. Conna Clark at the Philadelphia Museum told me how to go about getting prints and permissions. By far my greatest debt is to Neil Giordano, who did a masterful job of retrieving items from the rich store of images of Eakins' art; many people helped him, but two who went beyond the call were Barbara Grubb at Bryn Mawr and Barbara Katus at the Pennsylvania Academy of the Fine Arts.

My agent, Georges Borchardt, was an able ally. At Norton, which has been publishing my books for thirty-six years, my thanks go particularly to Starling Lawrence, a wonderfully skillful editor; his assistant, Morgen Van Vorst; and Anna Oler, who is designing what looks to be a beautiful book. Nancy Palmquist put me in touch with Trent Duffy, who has proved to be a superbly thorough and sensitive copy editor. Here in Wellfleet, Gloria Nardin Watts has given the manuscript scrupulous attention.

I got periodic boosts from my extended tribe in Ewing, Fort Washington, and Chappaqua. As always, Mary Drake McFeely was a wonderful reader. Last, there was Phil Hamburger. In visits to his study deep in the Wellfleet woods we egged each other on as he was working on his last book and I was working on this one. He was a great fan of Eakins and was determined that I write *Portrait*, which I dedicate to his memory.

WSM
Wellfleet, Massachusetts

INDEX

Page numbers in *italics* refer to illustrations.